Malchance:
From Walking to a Wheelchair

By

Jane Kryski

Published by Washington House
A division of Trident Media Company
801 N Pitt Street, Suite 123
Alexandria, VA 22314 USA

<u>An Ode to Mi Mam and Mi Pap</u>

I don't think you really understand how much of a basis my parents have been to me. My Mother's determination, for one thing, to get me to finish school was unbelievable. Through the Disability Center, there was this golf cart that would take you right up to the classroom door. I decided that I was going to assert my independence, and walk from this golf cart to the classroom. Of course, I couldn't do it alone because my balance is way too compromised and I would end up falling. So what did my Mother do? She walked with me into class and then did God knows what for an hour and a half until it was time to go. I have a caregiver now who is just floored at my mother's undying commitment. I used to take it for granted until I looked back at all that my Mother (and Father) have done. They are truly phenomenal. Now I am applying to school to get my Ph.D. See what they have started?

And my Dad. You don't hear much about him but oh my God. Could anyone be more loyal? My Mom says he is my greatest fan. We were born on the same day, so, there is an unbreakable bond. My Dad was always there. I am starting to cry now so, I won't go on. Just know that my parents are the greatest.

Once, while I was doing some adaptive skiing, I was telling my instructor (who is so cute) about my Mom. After meeting her, he said to me that she "rocked". In my eyes, my Mom holds the highest award.

Mama and Dada, this book is for you. Mainly Mama (Dada, you know I luv you), so I hope you enjoy. You certainly know the story.

Preface

It all started on February 9th, 1998. I was in Mont Blanc, France, and I had gone out the night before with some guys from Canada. They were working-class guys. I remember one guy, I think his name was Brice, but I'm not sure-the insignificant things get muddled into a little corner of your brain and they stay there never to see light again. Anyway, he patted me on the rear in this Australian bar that we went into and I thought it was the biggest thing. Funny what is considered BIG. All that seems unimportant now. Of course, I never saw the Canadian guys again but that doesn't matter right now. All that matters now is walking and getting my right hand not to scrunch up in a ball when I temporarily turn my attention somewhere else. I want the double vision fixed and I want the shunt out of my head. I want my hair back; all in all, I want my old life back.

Ok, I'm getting way ahead of myself. Let me get back to the Canadian guys again. So, I ended up eating with them in some small café. It wasn't too expensive but it was nice. So, before dinner we went to their room and drank a little red wine. I remember it being really hard to open the bottles but we finally got them open with a Swiss army knife and a regular butter knife. It's funny the things you remember when you look back! They walked me back to this apartment that I was staying in (with one boy from Israel, two girls from Mexico, and one girl from Greece) and I got ready for bed and climbed into my assigned dwelling spot for the week. At 4:00 in the morning I woke up with a terrible headache. I woke up and asked one of the girls from Mexico if she had two aspirins. She didn't have any but in retrospect I now realize that aspirin wouldn't have helped, I just needed a hospital-and right then. What followed I have no recollection of; it's just what my mom told me happened next. I guess I passed out and the kids took me into the bathroom and splashed some cold water on my face but that didn't do any good. The kids were quite bright and I thank my lucky stars for that. They called the paramedics and let them figure out what was wrong. Figuring out the 911 system in France is a feat in itself. The French are very bureaucratic and I figure that they are like that in everything they do. You see, one paper gets moved from one desk to the next. They were quite speedy in my case, though.

They thought it was a drug overdose at first but they can rest assured that it wasn't. I have never seen drugs, let alone tried them. It was up to the paramedics from that point on. At first they took me to a little mountain hospital but then they realized that it was something much more than just a little mountain hospital, could handle. So then they took me to Geneva, Switzerland. There they went in, and the brain surgery established that it was a bleed. But what they couldn't figure out was whether it was a cavernous hemangioma or an arterial venous malformation. What followed was a six-week coma and months of rehabilitation.

My mother and father were in the United States, and I didn't have their address and number in my address book. I mean who would, you don't think about the little things until they are past. Luckily, I had my brother's address in my address book and after a frenzied call from France he called my parents. When they heard they rushed over to Switzerland and set up camp in a local hotel. You see, my mom is very stoic but when you catch her in a situation that is somewhat emotional, having to do with animals or children, you will have a wreck on your hands. I'm not making myself very clear. You see, my mother will never say, "I love you", but she will cry like the dickens if you catch her in the right frame of mind. My father, on the other hand, is not very reserved but in this situation my father was the strong one. My mom says she can remember picking the hairs off of my clothes and crying, thinking that I was not going to live.

My father had to go back to work about two weeks after my initial accident. It wasn't an accident per se; it was only an accident because we didn't know it would happen. My Aunt Anne (Beanie) came over to Switzerland and stayed with my mother for about two weeks. One day they went on an expedition for hair barrettes. They searched high and low for hair barrettes that were big and not small like the ones that you will find in stores nowadays. They finally found a pair to their liking and I hold them close to my heart even to this day. That was when I had hair, though. I was soon to lose those beautiful locks that I treasured so much. I had hair below my shoulders, my bangs all grown out, and it was an attractive blond color. But that was no longer to be.

It was decided after about a month in Switzerland that I had to come back to the United States. My mother and aunt hired a doctor and a nurse and reserved five seats on an airplane. They got me back to San Francisco, and it turned out that I had viral meningitis. But the doctors at UCSF didn't realize this. Instead, they thought it was a malfunctioning French shunt (I had a shunt by this time).

They took it out and put it back in two more times until they realized that was not the problem. I can't imagine what my parents went through. Getting their daughter home from abroad on a stretcher only to find that she has viral meningitis. The thought makes me shudder.

I will cut right to the chase. What I had is called an arterial venous malformation. It is when an artery meets a vein with no capillary bed in between. It is not hereditary-rather, it was a fluke thing that chose to manifest itself while I was skiing in the Alps. It is such a fluke happening that my mother likens it to winning the lottery. We are, now, big partakers in the lottery.

If this whole ordeal had happened any other way I would feel cheated. I mean to say, that I was in the French Alps skiing. I got to see the world before my hemorrhage and I am eternally grateful for this.

I will always have double vision, a shunt in my head, a right hand that balls up, horrible circulation, terrible balance, and (oh, I can go on and on) I will always be in a wheelchair. But-the arterial venous malformation can never take away my memories of childhood and France.

i Jane Kryski Diary of Europe, September 13, 1997

Sept. 13, 1997 or, as the Europeans do it 13/9/97

Came to the airport with Mom, Karin (my sister), and Anne Marie (my cousin). (I met four other girls in my program, one of them Abi (UCB-from Australia), was born in England but lived in Australia for fourteen years and now lives in San Francisco. Her father is some big scientist who is world-renowned. Abi seems like a very fun girl. I can see us being good friends. Justine (UCSC from SF) is Abi's best friend. I don't get the best vibe from Justine but I bet she must just be nervous. Aimee (Boulder from Aptos) has a father who lives in Colorado and drives a Ferrari. Her mother lives in the Santa Cruz Mountains. Her parents are obviously divorced and she was regaling me with stories about her parents' custody battle over her sister and her. She stated, "My father is sending me to France to try and buy my love." OK. Marianne (UCD from San Jose) seems like the only grounded one. I guess that's not fair for me to say because they all seem like nice girls, but they just come from different backgrounds. For the most part, they are all very cool and fun-wild. We had all had sushi at the airport and Mom left. We got seats assigned at the end of the plane with two side by side- more legroom. Here we go!

9/14/97

The flight to Heathrow wasn't too bad. Abi and Justine got drunk off of red wine on the plane. When we got there we went to a pub and I had watermelon ale! It was pretty good. We had a four hour layover, so Abi, Justine, and I decided to experience our first "Smoker's Room"-totally disgusting. It left us smelling quite lovely. At the gate for Nice, we met other AIFS students, about 15. They are nice but not at all like my friends at home-I've noticed that a lot of the students have quite an eclectic background. Lots have already spent time or lived overseas for a lot of time in their lives. When I got on the plane to Nice I crashed. I was so tired. I was stuck in this shitty seat where the girl in front of me couldn't put her chair back because it keep hitting my knees. Damn long legs. God, I love them! To top that off I kept nodding off, asleep with my head tilted forward. Each time I woke up I would have this hideous crick in my neck-oh, it was hell! When we arrived in Nice, six students had lost their luggage. Luckily, I was not one of them, but my roommate, Marianne, was and she was very unhappy until she was reunited with it.

15/9/97

Last night I went to bed at 9:00 P.M. and didn't wake up until 7:00 A.M. It was great. I'm still exhausted because this weekend I didn't sleep for 36 hours. We had breakfast-great pain (bread) and café (coffee)! After our placement test we went into town-Cannes, where we are staying at an awesome college that seems more like a resort. Until we go to Paris, the college is so beautiful and there seems to be so much to do. It is an old, rectangular building with an unbelievable courtyard in the middle where students sit around and smoke cigarettes and drink coffee. I mean, does that sound like the life or what?

We walked around for four hours and had lunch at a patisserie. It was 13 F- a pear tart-my dad would be proud! We came back to the college at 3:00 and slept until dinner. After dinner, the four California girls shared two bottles of wine. So, at 10:30, I was pretty tired and a little drunk. I decided to be mature and go to bed-at least, for a nappy-poo. The nap turned out to be a bad idea because at 4:30 I was wide-awake. Ahhh!

16/9/97

First day of classes. Abby and Justine are hung over because after our wine they went out and picked up on French men until 4:00 A.M. They are definitely the cats out of our groupy. We call them "booty sluts", don't ask why!

Class was fine- I really like my professor-Sylvie. Marianne is in my class. We are in the advanced class. Oh yeah!

We had a Paris Academic meeting from 1-3 and then after that Marianne and I went into Cannes to change money, get a notebook, and pens. We ended up walking around for two hours. We saw the Festival de Film de Cannes- very intrusive and a tad out of place but a landmark nonetheless. We bought cheap beach towels and went to the beach.

It is very convenient because the college is right on the beach. I told you, this college is something! Marianne laid out and I went on a long swim. Pretty darn relaxing-swimming in La Cote d`Azur!

Downside of the day-we got homework. It's not too bad but since it's the first day of work, we figure we might have to go out and get a glass of wine-if I can stay up. I'm so tired and still jetlagged. Nice tomorrow, night yee-haw!

17/9/97

It's 8:10 A.M. and I had my alarm set for 7 A.M. so I could get up to call my parents and then go to a patisserie to get a palmier. Fat chance! We didn't get home until 2 A.M. last night. First we walked into town looking for a new bar. We couldn't find one so bashful me decided to ask three French guys. They were all macho and said, "Suivrez-nous." This means, "Follow us." We went to this expensive place/bar called Le Club Blue. I about fell over when I saw the prices. From what I hear, this is good for Paris. I guess I will go back to the States' poor. Tant Pis! So I ended up ordering a patis ricard for 50 F (10 dollars). Basically, this was the cheapest thing on the menu. But when we went to pay the bartender only charged me 16 F-Nice! Then we all went to Midnight Blue where Abi and Justine ordered us a mixture of beer and tequila. It sounds hideous but actually it is quite good. There were these cute young French guys there so we started talking to them. They were all 18-19, so we kind of lost interest. They were nice enough so they gave us a ride back to the college. It was so funny, with four girls in the backseat of a Mini-the shocks were squeaking.

All day today I have been exhausted. For some reason my jet lag has been especially bad- je ne sais pas! I took a three hour nap b/c I, knew we were going to Nice later on tonight.

The food here is lacking. I'm getting serious indigestion.

We left for Nice at 8:30 and when we got there our college guide walked us through the chic part of town and showed us all the pubs. We looked like a group of dorky tourists. Pretty funny! But we decided to go to "les 3 Diables." I got a Kir - that is like sweet red wine.

I'd like to drink more stuff, i.e., cocktails, etc., but I'm paranoid about getting fat. I have to make sure I watch my intake and try not to eat those delicious palmiers. I haven't had one yet but I can feel one coming tomorrow.

I need to go to bed. It's 2 a.m.-again- and I'm exhausted.

18/9/97

Today French class went well. We are speaking so much French I'll have to be fluent.

The food here is nasty and monotonous. I think tonight I'll go out and eat at a little cafe. Totally French-style.

I met a cool girl today named Lindsay. She has a house in Martha's Vineyard and invited me to visit. Uh, ok. We are going to get dinner sometime at a nice place.

One thing about this program is that most of the kids are well off. I was telling this guy Alex that a goal in my life is to have a house in Antibes (a very nice area in the Cote d'Azur) and Vail. He's like, "Oh, I have houses there." I was like, "Ya know." I secretly had eyes as big as saucers.

After class today we went to Antibes to visit the Picasso Museum. On the way we took the scenic route by the sea. It was so beautiful. I like Antibes so much more than Cannes. The water is more blue and the town is more provencal. The Musee was very nice. Obviously, Picasso had some works there along with other artistes. What was amazing was the view from the chateaux where the musee was located. Totally spectacular. We took such a long time in the musee b/c our guide explained almost every artist-in French of course!

After the musee we went and had crepes at this creperie. They were delicious. We are all very tired.

Tonight I am just going to read and relax and scope out a plan for Sunday.

19/9/97

I think I am the insomniac from hell. Last night I woke up at 12:45 and couldn't fall back to sleep until 3 A.M. The girls next door were loud and all of the cars and drunk kids coming home kept me awake. I ended up going to the phone booth and calling home at 2:30 but no one was there. Finally I got to bed. I took a nap for two hours and then called home. It was nice to talk to my mom and dad-and they sent me a letter. I sat in the courtyard with a coca light (Diet Coke) and read it. It was very relaxing. I tried to go running earlier but it was pretty hot so I only did it for half hour. I also booked a youth hostel in Monaco for tomorrow night. This nice girl Ashby and I are going to stay for sure. She is a southern belle who goes to school at an all women's college. Not an all girls-an all women's. She is very different. She is very small and not at all boisterous. I pride myself on knowing a lot about Miss Manners. I positively pale in comparison to Ashby. She is quite prim. I want to look into the Ballet de Monte Carlo but I think it will be too expensive. We'll see. Tonight we are going to go (hopefully) to a nightclub pour danser!

21/9/97

Where do I start? I luv Europe. After my run on Friday I took une petite nap. After that I showered and decided to go to a nightclub called Cat's Corner with the California girls. On the way we stopped at Midnight Blue for a desparado (beer and tequila) and a few cigarettes. It's funny b/c we are becoming regulars. We give the doorman the French hello-two kisses-one on each cheek. At about 11:30 we caught a taxi. We had to arrive in style b/c the scoop was that the doorwoman was a "canard" or a bitch. We arrived looking very good, chic. We got in but when I saw the cover charge I almost fell over-100F. Even though it included the first drink I thought it was expensive! This club was awesome, though. It was worth it for my first discotheque experience. When we got in they said we could have a table for only about half hr. b/c as it got later the tables were all reserved for the regulars. The interior was awesome-very modern. They had lots of American songs but at 1 A.M. the lights went off and the techno European beat came on. I started talking with two brothers from Sweden. Very good looking –John(ya-Juan) and Thomas. Hotties. I talked and danced with John the whole night. The smoke was unbearable. Everyone was just puffing away. My eyes couldn't take it anymore after 2:30. John and Thomas were going to Monaco to stay and golf and said they were going to call me (never did). I got the French goodbye from John-two kisses plus a big smacker right on the lips-cute, cute, cute. As we left we got whistles galore. I luv the French! We were quite drunk so we ate it up. A carload of guys in a Range Rover gave us a ride back to the college. One guy named Steve wanted to get together so I gave him my name and told him to call the college thinking he never would. Big mistake because he did. Five times by Monday. Luckily I have only gotten the messages. They were English and cute but still I don't think so. One perk is they have a table reserved at Cat's Corner which means they have connections & $. We'll see.

By the time we got home it was 3 A.M. and we had to be up at 8 A.M. to go to Monaco. I was thinking about not going but I'm glad I did b/c Monaco is absolutely beautiful–gorgeous. My friend Ashby and I decided we were going to stay the night so we booked a hostel. On the ride there Marianne et moi slept b/c we were so tired (she was a partaker in the previous night's escapade). When we arrived we got our tickets for the Musee d'Oceanagraphie and went to find the hostel. We decided not to tour the musee with the group b/c they are so annoying. They look like total tourists. Not my style. Some may call me a snob, tant pis! When we got to the hostel the women wouldn't let us check in for another half hr. so we ate our lunch on these narrow steep stairs that were very quaint and European. When we got back to the hostel at 12:00 the lady said she needed to see our passports if we wanted to stay. Marianne didn't bring her passport and the chick wouldn't let her stay. She was such a lazy-ass. We then decided to go to see the musee b/c Marianne now had to go back with the group. We thought it was very boring-lots and lots of preserved fish. This musee was internationally acclaimed but we were like "this stinks". Of course we later found out that there was a huge lower level with tons of fish. We missed it!

There were no signs or at least ones that we saw. Then we saw the palace but didn't go inside b/c the line was too long. We couldn't go in the cathedral b/c there was a wedding taking place. I now want to get married in Monaco. Honestly, there is not a bad part of town. After that we went to a café and had a café (imagine that) avec une salade de fruits. It was very inter-national. Our waiter was this cute French guy who kept telling me "Tu es charmante." It was a lot of fun. Marianne went back to the group and Ashby and I decided to go to find a hairdryer. We go to Monaco and what do we do? The necessity, of course. This task took us all over Monaco-we did it all-mastered the bus system, saw the casinos, and made reservations at the elegant Café de Paris in Monte Carl.

After all of this we decided to go back to the hostel and take a nap. Oh man-when we got to our room we were shocked and terrified. Can you say "shithole?" There were four people to a room and no sheets and the mattress (or foam pad) was filthy. Poor Ashby kept saying "oh no" in her cute southern accent. The two other girls staying with us were from Scotland. We took a taxi to dinner and had about an hour to kill so we went to le Bar American in the Hotel de Paris. Very posh. We were the youngest people there and we kept getting looks. This old lady from Monaco was sitting next to us and was telling us how nice we were and she kept feeding us her h'ors d'oeurves. I liked her.

Dinner was fabulous. I had salmon and we people watched. All the beautiful people from around the world were there. It was very expensive (500 franc) and at the end Ashby said she was so glad that she had found a friend to go out with that she wanted to pay for dinner. I was like "no way" but she insisted. It was very nice of her. All in all, it was a fun evening. We took a taxi home-to the hostel, and for part of the payment the taxi driver said we had to give him a kiss on the cheeks-pretty funny.

I forgot to write about the casino. After dinner we decided to try to get in the casino. You have to be 21 and we heard that they usually checked your passport. They didn't with us so were able to walk right in. It was such fun. We spent 50 F-won a little but in the end lost it all. As we were ready to leave this older Frenchman started slipping us more francs to gamble with. That ended so we left.

The hostel was ok. I didn't sleep well so it was nice when were able to leave this morning, We were having a café this morning and before we left Monaco this American guy came up and asked us if there was an ATM near. It ends up that he went to Menlo and then Cal. He was nice and his name was Andy. I told him to find me at my sorority house if he was ever in Davis.

Ashby and I caught the train and I have taken naps all day.

22/9/97

I had trouble sleeping last night. I was starving so I had trouble sleeping. This morning I drank enough coffee to keep myself awake. After class we went to Grasse.

The guy Alex who has the houses in Vail and Antibes said he was going to take us on his boat but he totally flaked on us. Instead we walked into town to catch a bus to Grasse. It was took about half an hour to get there. Grasse is the perfume capitol of the world. We walked to the Frambourg Factory. I got some beautiful perfumes for gifts and one perfume called Soliel for myself.

After that we went to the International Musee de Perfume. It was not that interesting. 12 F down the drain. After that we went to the Moliere Factory-another tour and more walking. We then went back to Cannes and when we arrived we set out to find the Poste and mail some letters.

What an ordeal! I was so tired that I couldn't understand anyone at all. After I got the letters mailed Ashby and I decided to go to dinner at a petite café. Very nice. I had a salad Nicoise and a crème caramel (fabulous) at a little place called Café Mokita. When we walked back to the college I found that the English guy, Steve, in the Land Rover had called again-thank God I wasn't here to take his call-he definitely scares me.

Oh well -Abi, Jus and Marianne had gone to get wine so I had a few glasses with them before I did my homework and went to bed. I think I may call Liv tonight. We'll see!

23/9/97

Today we went to Ille St. Margarite which is about 30 minutes in a ferry from Cannes.

The only downfall of the day is that the English guy Steve, called again two times. What a god dammed stalker! It is really beginning to scare me. I finally asked the college to tell him that I had left. It really put a cloud over my day. The island was beautiful anyway. We walked all around it. Walked and walked and walked-that's all I seem to do lately! It was crazy. We were walking around this woodsy island and all of a sudden there is this clearing and, voila, a café. Right in the middle of nowhere on the far end of the island.

We stopped and had an Orangina, etc. We then caught the ferry back. In Cannes there were all these nice yachts and boats and we found out there was a regatta going on. Talk about hottie, hottie men! We decided to walk and take a look at the scenery. Nice guys from all over-even New Jersey. But I had to go under cover because we saw the infamous Range Rover.

We went back to the college and had dinner-quite disgusting. I'm just in a bad mood and tired so I called home except no one was there. Quelle dommage! I think my new camera might be broken so I'm going to try and fix it soon and then go to bed. We are going to Nice tomorrow and I need to be rejuvenated.

25/9/97

Yesterday we went to the Museum of Modern Art in Nice. It was really boring-I can't stand modern art. Anyway, Ashby's mom is in the hospital ICU because she has heart problems. She is very worried-so when we got to the musee we just went to the café and got a tart. It wasn't very good. So next time I'm in Nice I am not going to St. Paul to see modern art!

Ashby was telling me that her aunt who is 6'2" and who works for Elite Models wants to meet me. I don't know-we'll see. I would luv to see the Elite office and all the glitz,etc. After the musee we went back to the college and I decided to call home-it was so nice to talk to my mom. I was talking so fast- I just had so much to say. I was pleasantly (ok-ecstatic) surprised because mom said my dad booked me a ticket home for Christmas! Yeah!

After that I was in a good mood so Ashby and I went to get a glass of red wine. We took a stroll down by the regatta. Oh lord, the men were so hot! All nice and showered. September is the month to come to Cannes! I really want to come back. Anyway, I think tonight we may go down and try to party with them. On verra! (We'll see)

27/9/97

Today after class we had a long meeting about our departure to Paris. Before, in class, we took a long test and I did perfectly on the written part. It is a satisfactory feeling to know that my French is improving.

The rest of the day we just packed our suitcases because they had to be ready in the courtyard by 2:00 on Friday. Not fun. Luckily I was able to fit all my clothes in with some room to spare-how? I don't know.

On Thursday night we had a crepe soiree and party at the college. The crepe was good. It was so funny to watch the

European men at work. They all look gay. Tight pants and shirts and dancing where everyone could see them. Such macks! At the college there are more girls than guys so they totally make out. Anyway, this German guy named Roger was getting everyone's address. As he was getting mine this little German girl came up and started kissing him and biting his neck. It was hilarious! Later, after she walked away, he said, " I don't have to warm her up because she is ready to go all night." It was classic!

On Friday morning we bought our teacher flowers and chocolate. She is so cute-I luv Sylvie (our teacher)! She was so pleased that she whipped out the chocolates and gave us all one. She is tan, thin with blue eyes, extremely nice. She is very classic.

When class was over I took a huge nap in order to get ready for the night. At 7:30 we went to dinner. It was a group of seven girls: Gillian and Emily (from New York), Marianne, Abi, and Justine. Maybe just six girls. We were all dressed up and looking good. We went to Old Cannes (Vieille Cannes). It's a little street filled with nice provincial restaurants. We ate at a place called L'Assiette, which was semi-expensive but definitely worth it.

I had salade de la Mer, le loup, and citron sorbet. Very good! After dinner we walked to Midnight Blue where the exact same band was playing the exact same songs as Wednesday night. Fun, though! A lot of people from college were there, but it was fun. My friend Dave paid me 40 F not to smoke cigarettes for the rest of the night! He rationalized it by saying he was saving a few days of my life. We'll see!

This morning we woke up at 9 A.M. to some cleaning lady knocking on our door telling us to get the hell out. When I didn't get up she walked into our room and said, "Jeune fille, se reveille" I was all "Non, non, je dois dormir encore" (No, no I must sleep more). She just said we had to out by 10:00. What a bitch! It was kind of funny, though.

So right now I am on the TGV on the way to Paris-A whole new adventure in itself!

16

It is about 11P.M. and I am reclining in a double bed with a white fluffy comforter-I like it! The TGV ride was long-six hours, but we finally arrived in Paris. The station was a mess!

American Institute for Foreign Study (AIFS) students were all over trying to get their luggage from SNCF. The staff then proceeded to hand out white envelopes with our addresses and put us in a taxi. It was rather scary because I had no idea what to expect. And of course I had the psycho taxi driver from hell who wanted me to give him English lessons and wants my telephone number. Oh sure! Anyway, I arrived with my 15 bags and Madame de la Baume (my house mom) came downstairs. She is an old lady with a limp-extremely nice. When I came upstairs she had pain, sausisson, and une petite salad. We dined together and chatted, in French of course. She only knew one word in English-strawberry!

She has three kids and a couple of grandkids-one of which is my age and is named Celine-who lives with her during the school year or something like that-I couldn't quite understand.

I then unpacked, and I am in bed right now trying to figure out where the hell I am in this city!

9/30/97

Okay, look at me! This situation is probably the best possible! I have my own phone, own TV, own bathroom-life is good, very good. On Monday morning I braved the metro on my own and went for my first orientation meeting. Harrowing, but I did it!

We got the info for our classes, etc., and our mail. I got two letters from Liv (my best friend from college), one from Susi (my best friend from home who is studying in Florence, Italy), one from Katie (my cousin), and a message from Dr. Juan Lopez-this heart surgeon that I met in San Francisco at the French Embassy. I will talk more about him later.

Anyway, after the meeting all of the girls (the six of us who went to dinner in Cannes) took the metro to an ultra savvy part of Paris the Champs d'Elysee. We lunched at a café and walked around some more.

Everything around the Champs d`Ellyse is very expensive!

At 2:00 we met at the Me Trocadero shops to go on a bus tour. AIFS provided that for us, so I wasn't about to miss it!

We saw every imaginable sight. It was quite informative, but also quite long. The most expensive shopping is around Rue de la Paris which is near la Place de l`Opera. The really famous jewelry stores are all around there also!

We also saw the Ritz where Princess Di had her last meal. As we were passing in front of the Ritz our bus hit a taxi-chaos ensued. It was pretty funny! The drivers were tall talking fast. I had no idea what they were saying, but I knew it couldn't be good!

After the tour I decided to walk home. We were let out near the Tour d`Eiffel. I decided to get a few shots of the Tour d`Eiffel. I felt like a total tourist but it had to be done. At that point I separated myself from the group.

After three cups of coffee (in the true French style) I was getting very impatient. Everyone was taking too long to decide what to do. I took off in the direction of the Tour d`Eiffel. As I was walking towards it these guys came near me and one stuck his hand under my dress. It was terrible! I smacked him with my book bag and started power walking—better. I felt so violated. Is that how the French operate?

Anyway, I walked under the Tour d`Eiffel and around the gardens towards the Ecole Militaire. The weather in Paris has just been perfect for this type of stuff-about 80 degrees F-very abnormal for this time of year. My house is down the road from the Metro La Motte Piquet and directly across from M-Cabaronne. Great LOCATION!

When I got back I had a Palmier and an ice tea. There is a great bakery across the street and a perfect park across the street where I was able to study my French because we have our placement test soon. When I got back I called home to Olivia and Italy to Susi. Susi and I have tentative plans for Paris, Italy, and Switzerland. I'm very excited!

At 7 P.M. I met Ashby who came strutting up in leather-yes leather pants. She looked like a new woman-not as proper as before. I luv it! We had dinner in a café across from the wine store Nicolas and parallel to l'Ecole Militaire. I had a tomato salad- it was great. After dinner we said our French goodbye and walked away like true Parisiennes.

This morning we all met at Rue Raspail to take the entrance exam. It was not long or hard. After that Marianne and Ashby and I were going to walk around but this annoying girl Tiama latched on and asked if she could come with –ugh! Marianne then decided to go with Abi and Justine and we told Tiama we were going to go home- we lied. Let me tell you a little about her. OK, she comes from Nebraska-of all places-and she says she has an Elite modeling contract in New York, Chicago, and Dallas. RIGHT!

Instead we took off towards the Boulevard Saint Michelle! It is awesome! I luv it! There are so many more young people to see. And guess what, I did it, I ordered leather pants. They fit like levis but they are ordering them 10 centimeters longer! I'm so excited b/c they come in next Thursday-yeah.

After that we went to the Latin Quarter, fun, oh geey (this spelling??) to eat sushi- lots of fun. All these different resto euc and jewelry stores-I liked it. Ashby and I had a snack at a patisserie and then continued to walk all over the city. We saw Notre Dame and Ile St. Louis and Ile de la Cite` Great day, lots of walking!

———————————Munich this weekend———————————

10/1/97 White Rabbit

Okay, I think I'm going to die from fatigue! This morning I met Marianne at a café near the Sorbonne. At 9:00 we got together and discussed which classes we would take that could possibly transfer for UCD. After that we strolled down to the Sorbonne and registered. It turns out that I placed extremely high on my test. I am able to take regular French courses as well as the French Business Course which I will hopefully be able to get a certificate in- I am a happy girl!

After that we walked down the Boul St. Michel and looked

in shops, etc. We were starving so we ate lunch at this Greek Place in the Latin Quarter. It was very good! Only downfall was that the girls I was with were so rude. It was incredible. We decided to separate and Marianne, Ashby, and I went to the AIFS office to get our mail and after that we had a Cocoa Light in a little brasserie.

Marianne and I then decided to book a couchette for the girls. I was a little worried because it was 90F each but I paid for the girls. I hope I get paid back! I decided to check out gyms after that-way expensive-almost $400 for three months. We'll have to see about that!

I went home and chatted with Madame de la Baume and her sister, Isabelle. They invited me to dinner tomorrow. We're going to have "froid de veau." I'm a little nervous because I think it's cold meat!

At 6:15 I was supposed to meet Ashby but I got incredibly turned around on the metro and ended up being thirty minutes late- luckily she was still waiting for me. When I finally got there-the St Phillippe de Rue stop- we started to walk around. It is a very nice area of Paris, lots of nice boutiques and upper scale men's stores. Somehow we got to the Sacre Coeur (I think) and had dinner at a little café in front. Service was slow at La Pepiniere and the food was just OK but hottie, hottie, French boys sitting next to us! Oh Mon Dieu! I asked one directions and I almost fainted! Too bad I had no idea what he told me so of course we got lost again.

Somehow we got to the Hotel des Invalides and some other nice boys walked us home. My feet hurt sooo badly!

Off to Munich at 10:30 P.M.!

5/10/97

It is Sunday morning and I just got back from Munich- Oktoberfest was so awesome! We took the couchette on Thursday evening and arrived there on Friday morning–along with every other American staying in Europe. We met so many people who knew friends of friends, etc. We decided to search for a room and finally found two doubles in one hotel one double in a hotel across the street. Ours was Hotel Mueie and it was 185 Marks a night including breakfast-pretty good deal considering we had no reservations and it was Oktoberfest.

After we got settled we took off towards Oktoberfest. We got there at 11 A.M. and it was already out of control-huge buildings filled with people drinking beer, eating chickens, and singing songs. There were hardly any seats left at all!

Chad, this guy from New Jersey who was also with AIFS, and I managed to find a table in the Pilsner House. It was only 12:00 and every table was taken. If you want to get a good spot you have to go early and keep it all day b/c everyone is so drunk by 10 A.M. that they don't move and after (around 2:00) they all stumble home! After Chad and I got the table the others came to sit down and we took off to scout out Oktoberfest.

Huge. Awesome. Out of control! They are some descriptive words for Oktoberfest. We stopped at Hofbrau haus and had a liter of beer. NOT being a beer drinker, that was a lot for me. We sat next to these young beefy Germans (on one side) and this other chic middle-aged couple on the other. They (all of them) decided to take us under their wing and teach us some beer cheers and dances to do while standing on tables- lots of fun.

We then left and followed some other German kids around who were going to show us the cool place to go. This was about 4:00 (so it was clearing out, sort of). By that time, there was some sort of bomb scare and we couldn't get into anymore of the beer halls. So instead we headed back to our seats in the Pilsner hall. The man at the door wasn't going to let us in but I told him I was from California-enough said!

Came back to our friends and drank more beer and met a cute German named Alexander. All he could say was "Agh, Jane, you are a vonderful voman!" I ended up kissing him but when he signed to come home with him I said, "No." That is universal isn't it? I am happy I played the prude.

The next morning we woke up and had a fabulous buffet. We met up with Justine and Emily (one of our crew) who were staying in another hotel and we decided to go to Daschu to see the concentration camp.

That was a very sobering experience. The suffering that those people endured was unreal. We were able to join an English tour that was quite interesting. The actual camp is all reconstructed except for the crematorium-which I declined from seeing. I bought a book written by a priest in the camp. I'm very excited about reading it. Am I a dork?

We spent about four hours there and after that went back to Munich and walked around downtown. Absolutely beautiful. I wish I had more time to spend there because there is so much to see. We had to catch the 9 P.M. train back to Paris. We barely made it- about one minute to spare. There were six of us in the compartment-cramped. It was hard to sleep because it was cold and swaying, and some loud, drunk Germans took over the control room and the loudspeaker. They proceeded to sing beer songs for 20 min (at 2 A.M.). The train abruptly stopped at which point I think they were thrown off! So, to say the least, we didn't get a lot of sleep.

When we got back to Paris we decided to meet back up later to see the Sacre Coeur.

When we got there, it was a lot of people being disrespectful to the church. We also saw the Dali Museum. I think he was crazy-not my style-at all. I came home after that and Madame had bought me a Palmier-what a babe!

P.S. My friends are giving me shit about Alexander. They call him Lederhausen boy! Oh well!

October 7th, 1997
On Monday I was able to get out of bed and go running. I'm happy to say that I didn't cough up a lung. I wasn't a smoker until I came to Paris. Everyone smokes here! I might as well be one of the many.

After that I met some friends at Place de l'Opera and we went and had lunch at a little café called Cafe Mondial right near Gallery Lafayette. I decided that I needed a raincoat so I braved the gallery and got one. It is very cute-black patent leather with a tie around the waist and a big collar-I luv it!

At about 4:00 I went to the American University to take a class in politics. The prof's name is John Lee. He did postgraduate work at Harvard, Notre Dame and Georgetown. He was quite impressive. I don't think I am going to be able to take it though. I feel that while I'm here I need to concentrate on my French. The course really would have taught me a lot but there was a twenty page paper 2-4 pagers, two oral and two written exams. Quite challenging. I-quite frankly-don't want to work that hard. Martha Dwyer (our AFIS overseer) said I would have my hands full with other French coursework. On verra!

On Monday night a group of us went to a fondue place on 17 rue de 3 freres. They served the wine in baby bottles. It was a lot of fun. While we were eating, it started pouring (of course, I didn't bring my raincoat). Me-being the bashful person that I am-struck up a conversation with this guy I thought was cute. It turns out that his name is Marcel and he is a divorcee and he is from Marseilles and the clincher-he was 5 foot 4 inches. I couldn't tell until he stood up. I was thinking, good God. I was like, "No way." I turned disinterested quite quickly.

He said he had some good hash. I'm not into that but a lot of my friends are. So, after we got thoroughly drenched and my friends got high, we parted ways. Marianne was pretty drunk-those damn baby bottles- so I walked her home and took a taxi back to my place.

Remember- It was very hot inside the restaurant so next time, dress lightly.

Today I got to AIFS early in order to sign myself up for all of the cultural events. I'm excited because I'll be going to the opera, ballet, theatre, plus more. Yeah!

After that I walked with Dave to the American University. I had to go to a boot shop because both my heels broke off my boots-pieces of crud! I was running down from the restaurant with my high friends and it was all cobblestone and I guess the boots weren't meant for cobblestone. Oh well, it's all part of living.

I then came home and napped. But not for long, because, Susi called and we finalized our plans for Paris and Italy, can't wait!

Sushi for dinner, yum, in Latin Quarter. I also forgot to mention that Dr. Lopez called me this morning. He wants to come see me in Paris. Is this man crazy?! I told him I had a boyfriend but he said he just wants to get to know me. He seems harmless but I am definitely on my guard. I told him that if he wanted to see me when he was in Paris that would be fine but I told him not to make a special trip to see me. I bet he wants action-whatever!

Let me fill you in on Dr. Juan. I was in San Francisco at the French Embassy. I was getting my visa for France (obviously) and he was getting a visitor's visa for Martinique. Normally you wouldn't have to get a visitor's visa but he isn't a U.S. citizen. He took quite a liking to me. Can you really blame him? Let's face it-when you've got it you've got it!

*Just five minutes ago Auntie Pam's sister Karen and her husband Dick called and we are going to get together tomorrow night to go out. Fun!

9/10/97

First day of classes was yesterday. It's about time! I am in Niveau Supervieor Economics-which means I will be able to take a test and hopefully obtain a business certificate. My teacher's name is Jean-Francois Hans. He is a big dork but very enthusiastic about teaching.

After class a friend, Dave, and I went to buy our books and then I went to a café and wrote a few letters. The metro was on strike so the trains weren't running that often. There were long waits and lots of people. When I finally got home I had to get ready to go out with Karen and Dick. They are staying in the 18th arrondisment so I had to leave early because the trip requires two metro stops-with the strike it could be a pain.

I got to the area early so I bought them a little bottle of Beaujolais. We ended up going to a Greek place in the Latin Quarter. We had a great meal and they were fun to talk to. It surprised me how well traveled Karen and Dick are. They have been everywhere. One thing I did notice was that Dick is very money oriented-always likes a deal. We all might get together again-fun! They are ultra cool!

Today I had to sign up for my phonetics class-boring. The weather was unusually warm and balmy. Of course, I was dressed for a snowstorm. I was sweating so much!

After class I picked up my leather pants. You know what? Those pricks charged me 50 francs extra for the 10 cm extra of fabric. I was ticked off! After that I decided to walk along the Seine. It was windy but nice to walk around and just people watch.

I found a very nice area near the Musee d 'Orsay and the Rue des Beshelles. Dinner with Ashby tonight and maybe a bar!

10/10/97
My feet are killing me! Ahhhhhhhh! Must write tomorrow. It's 3:30 and I just got home from Les Bains Douche-an ultra hip night club in the Bastille.

10/10/97-later in the morning
The other night I met Ashby and we went to our favorite café-the Café Suffren. It has great seafood salads and the atmosphere is nice and lively. I had my leather pants on. We had a lot of fun. Afterwards we went to the Buddha Bar- a very chic bar right next to L'Hotel de Crillon. We swaggered in and sat down. It was very dark inside and the chairs were very low to the ground, without backrests. I had a kir. There was this guy sitting alone at a table with chairs with backs. He started talking to us so we switched tables and sat with him. He didn't have a drink and he was constantly fidgeting-probably drugs. After we sat down with him the waitress became very rude and said we had to leave soon because the black guys' table was reserved. He got all weird and took off without even having a drink. Ashby complained to the manager about the rudeness of our waitress. The manager said something about the French being racist. All in all, the experience was VERY weird. I like

to think that he was some big drug lord on the run. Hey, there's nothing like beefing up a story!

The next morning I got up and went to my 1st painting analization class. Pretty boring! The weather was still a little balmy but it rained the whole morning and got a little colder at night. I went to Monoprix (a store like Target) and bought some groceries. We thought we might go out so I wanted to rest a little before we did. Of course, just as I wanted to rest the phone started ringing. I've been named the official planner so everyone was calling me to figure out where we are going to go.

Juan Lopez called also. He said that this summer he was going to come and buy all my watermelons (I was the water-melon queen-selling watermelons at local Farmer's Markets) so he could have a watermelon party. He said he really wants to get to know me-blah,blah, blah, I have no idea what he expects.

Anyway, we all met at 10:00 and went to the Bastille for drinks. It was wild and crazy. We definitely need to go back. Ashby and I lost the others and stumbled into a bar called Havana next to The Banjo. It was a fun Latin type bar. We were standing up and this extremely hot French guy came up and gave me a kiss and welcomed me to France. Thanks, I am glad to be here!

We sat down with him and were talking to his friends. He was definitely hot but weird too so we left after a while. We found our friends again at a bar called Sans Sanz-fun. We wanted to go dancing and we had to get there before the metro stopped, so we left and headed to Les Bains.

We arrived at Les Bains Douche at 12:30. There was a line but we got in easily enough. It was 120F to get in and another ten at the coat check. I didn't have to pay this the other night. When it is YOUR money, then it is harder to spend!

At first when we got in, I was hot and claustrophobic and I wanted to leave. I met this guy Tarig who's a journalist for La Tribune. He was nice and he said that a famous D.J. was playing-named Doug Something and he was from New York. At 2:00 it got crowded and lots of people were dancing. It got a lot better but I still didn't know any of the songs since they were European. If I thought it was crowded before…I was just waiting for someone to yell, "Fire." Thought: It's harder to dance to unknown songs than you think.

At 3:00 we left and tried unsuccessfully to hail a Taxi. Finally two guys gave us ride home. It's so weird because everyone smokes pot here. They just whipped it out while driving around. I was like," No thanks."

Woke up the next morning feeling like shit. Went to see Napoleon's Tomb and after that called Shane (Chad's best friend and roommate) and Chad. They wanted to see a movie so we went to dinner at 8:00. Great little Italian place off the Metro Mabillon. A definite return visit. Saw L.A. Confidential afterwards. Very good.

10/12/97
Vieu-le-Vicomte and Fountainbleu today. Tired and sick. Madame went to dinner so I got to watch TV all night! Yes!

13/10/97
Today was a very long day! I had to be in class at 9:00 so I was up at 7:30. That wasn't too bad but the temperature had dropped about 15 degrees since yesterday. It was sooo cold today! I went to my Societe Francaise class which was two and a half hours of a teacher talking really quickly in French. After that I went outside and almost died (am I dramatic or what) because it was so cold! So I went and bought a scarf for 22F and mittens for 15F. That is probably my best deal in Paris so far! And better yet, I was toasty warm afterwards.

After Cours Practique I went with Shane and Chad and had lunch at a French place in the Latin Quarter. We talked about Interlocken, Switzerland (where we were going that weekend). At lunch, I had onion soup. It was very tasty. After lunch I went to Rue d' Ecoles in order to pick up my livre jaun and then I went up to Rue l'Estrope to sign up for my conference. When I got there the woman talked me into two conferences telling me that I could get a diplome that way. She was very pushy-now I have five classes and I don't know what to do! I am going to call Martha Dwyer tomorrow and see what she has to say about all of this. I'm rather worried.

Dave and I were supposed to study but he has to get up at 5:00 to go to Brussels. So that was out. I ended up just going home.

Ashby called and we chatted. Then Marianne called to see if I wanted to go to dinner with everyone. I just wasn't in the mood so I decided not to go. I bought a bottle of wine so I opened that up and had a glass. As I was pouring, it Caroline, who is a sorority sister and a friend from Davis, called and she was very excited when I told her that I would be in Madrid for New Year's Eve. All she could say was, "We're going to have fun." I believe her!

After I told Caroline I was drinking wine alone she said I needed a boyfriend. I told her I knew that and hung up. I feel lame now!

16/10/97

After I finished writing in my journal last night, Chad and Shane called and we went to a movie. On Tuesday told Monsieur Hans that I had a rendezvous chez docteur so I left class at 1:30. Of course I didn't have a doctor's appointment instead Shane and I went to Giverny to see Monet's house and gardens-The gardens were beautiful and the ponds looked just as I thought. But there were so many tourists-all American and Japanese.

Monet's house was not that impressive. Only two rooms were showed to us and none of the paintings in the house were authentic.

When I left Giverny I had to meet Karen and Dick on the Champs Elysees. We went to dinner at a nice place called Chez Clement. Very nice! At the end Karen gave me two packs of cigarettes because she said she knew they were expensive! Cool, I'm going to visit them when I return to the States.

Yesterday, I woke up and it was pouring rain. I was just about ready to leave to go view the Montparnasse Tower with AIFS when Kirk called. Wilson and Palmer were with him. They are some of my best friends from Davis. It was so great to talk with them. Wilson, the flake that she is, isn't coming to visit. She hadn't even worked into a ticket yet-ahhh. It makes me so mad!

When I got off the phone with them I ran out the door. It was pouring. When I got to Montparnasse we zoomed up to the top. Of course, there was no visibility so we had a café. At 11:00 all the clouds lifted and we could see all of Paris. It was amazing!

Chad and I went to class and after got a falafell in the Latin Quarter. Yummy! At 4:30, Marianne, Abi, and Justine came over and we watched t.v. chez moi. It was fun!

At 8 P.M., we all met again at a place called Chartier to have dinner. It was an extremely cheap dinner and not so good. Go figure! Will write more later.

20/10/97

I am on my way home from an incredible weekend! Interlaken, Switzerland, is where I want to live.

Okay: on Thursday I figured out why I had not gotten any mail. It turns out that I had given everyone my address but I forgot to tell them to write "Chez Madame de la Baume, so the ass down at the bottom of the apartment sent them all back. It is so frustrating because he knew that Madame houses American students. Last year, she had a girl from San Diego for eight months. The guy had also seen me come in and go out about 50 times but he still could not go out of his way to call Madame and see if the mail could be mine. He is such a turd!

Thursday afternoon I met Dave and we went to the happy hour at the American Institute. It was fun but kind of the same old bar scene. I had to leave b/c at 8:00 I had dinner with Madame and Isabella her daughter. Madame cooks huge pieces of meat and is insulted if I don't eat it all. It was a good dinner nonetheless.

On Friday, I went to class at 12:00 but I thought I would try to take the bus. I ended up in wherever. I thought we were going to Opera to change money but the bus took me somewhere near the Gare du Nord. I ended up walking 25 blocks to the Opera and by the time I got there I had to get on the metro to go to class. After class, I ran home to get my bag to head off to Switzerland. When we finally got to the train station it turns out that all the trains were totally full. We needed reservations, but of course we didn't have any because we were idiots. Did we know?

I talked to three conductors. The first two were asses and finally the last one let us on! I told him I was studying here from California. Enough said.

When we got on the train Justine and I went to get food. I bought a fruit sorbet for 23 francs. There were four pieces of fruit. Each piece of fruit cost 5 francs. After I asked for four plastic cups and the jerk at the counter would not give them to us. I even told him I was from California. No cigar!

I was so pissed! I ended up taking two cups from a dirty plate. I cleaned them off and poured two cups of wine for Chad and Shane (shh! they don't know) and Justine and I used my fruit salad container.

We finished one bottle of wine and we tried to open the second one but it was really hard. By this time we were laughing A LOT. Chad tried so hard to open the wine that his head turned red. We ended up not being able to get the cork out so we had to push it through. It took us about half hr. and everyone around us was laughing at us and trying to help us. Crazy!

We got to Bern and we thought we were going to have to get a schedule and have a huge layover. When we got off the train we were running around the train station running into each other with our backpacks and Chad was yelling at us to cut it out. Disclaimer: We were pretty drunk.

We were running right next to a train with Interlaken written on it, so we jumped on. We ended up not having a layover at all!

We got into Interlaken and followed the signs for Balmer's

(where we were staying). We got there and ended up rooming with four girls from Dijon. After we got settled in we headed down to the bar (the whole basement). We had a couple of beers and got a tad drunk. I went up about a half an hour before the others. When they came up they were so drunk. We got up on our bunks (two per person). Justine went to get extra pillows in the next room and fell off the ladder and got lost coming back to our room. It was so funny that we couldn't stop laughing. We were snorting and giggling and then Shane busts out with, "Be quiet or else you will wake up the Mustard Girls." Of course they heard it but they luved the name!

The next morning we got up and went to book paragliding but it was full so we signed up for glacier climbing for the next day. So instead we went to a store and bakeri and bought an incredibly cheap lunch. We then took the train to other water-falls. They were in these caves. The water came down the inside of this mountain. It was incredible, to say the least!

After the waterfalls, we walked to a town called Stilhoun and along the way we had lunch on the banks of a river. Justine got stung on the finger by stinging nettles and then we took pictures by some cows nearby. It was wonderful!

We continued on to the town and watched people bungy jumping from 590 feet! Scary! We ended up taking the tram up to 11,000 feet to the top of Stilhorn. The view was like no other! When we came down the mountain we had dinner at an Italian place. The food wasn't that good, the prices were high, and the service was terrible. Great choice!

We went back to Balmer's and went to the bar. I bought this Australian guy, named Matt, a drink. He invited me to a party in London on the 1st of November.

The next morning we got up-very sleepy! Got in the car to go climbing and I got stuck in the front seat. The guy who was driving named me the co-pilot and called me Janie-lien. The ride up took an hour and on the way I fed this guy five crois-sants and about a liter of coffee! I was amazed! I was trying to figure out how much this guy could eat.

When we got up there I met a nice guy named Mike from San Diego. Very cute and smart. We climbed next to each other on the hour ascent. It was a lot of work but so worth it when we finally reached the top. At the top, we had lunch and set up for the glacier climbing part. It was the most fascinating thing that I have ever done. I can't really describe it in words other than that it was an experience of a lifetime.

It was so much work and it was hard because you had to stick your crampons into the ice. I was shaking from muscle fatigue. Why am I such a wimp? The hard part was trusting the crampons because instinct told you that they wouldn't hold, but they did. Repelling down was also awesome!

Coming down was also a lot easier. When we got in the van we drove for about ten minutes and then made a rest stop. I had a drink with Mike. He bought it for me. He was so nice! I am kicking myself for not getting his number!

When we were going back we kept seeing signs for Assenfurt. We were joking about the name and then Shane says, "Wow, this town is big." But Assenfurt meant exit! It was so funny!

When we got back to Interlaken they had bread and cheese and beer for us! It really topped the day off! You couldn't have asked for a better day-the weather was phenomenal and the group we went with was awesome!

The train ride home was sad. No one wanted to leave!

Best weekend so far!

Weekend Highlights

Wine on Train-bottle that wouldn't open
McDow's-Biracial Barbi
Donkey Poster-imitating the donkies
Balmer's Bar
Lunch by River-Justine getting stung by stinging nettles
View from Stilhorn
Steam rolling at night/Justine getting lost
Mustard Girls
Glacier climbing-all day

Drink with Mike
Balmer's and Interlaken!

23/10/97

This week has just flown by! Tuesday night we had our wine course which was informative. The metro broke so I was half hr. late. I had to take the bus with about 200 other people. We were packed in like sardines! The highpoint of the day was that I had East Indian food for lunch. I luv East Indian food! You see, I am from Yuba City which has the third-largest population of Indians in the world. I can't help but like it, it is my culture. There are tons of East Indian places right off of Me Strasbourg St. Denis. So cheap too! Note: Me stands for Metro.

After our wine course Abi, Justine, and I went out for a drink. We got off at Me Concord and the only bars were these sleazy x-rated bars. We finally found a semi-normal one where we had a few drinks and a croque-monsieur-my first one! They are like a grilled cheese with ham. They are so good. Almost ecstasy. Afterwards, Abi and I were semi-drunk so we got a crepe. Bon! It was a high fat night. Oh well, you only live one time and I plan to make this time worth it!

My boots broke again so I went to Zara International and bought a really nice pair for 85 dollars. The next day I caught my foot on something and poked a hole in them-I was so mad! The French seem to be really rude this week and I can't completely deal with it right now. The reason I feel this way is because I did go back to Zara and they gave me a new pair but not without a lot of hassle. The chick was so condescending, to me I wanted to pop her hard. But I refrained because what I really wanted was a new pair of boots. I just kept my mouth shut! It was hard, but I did it!

Susi is coming next Tuesday so I booked her hostel at a place called Young and Happy right off of Me Place Monge. It's in a really fun part of town in the Latin Quarter. I skipped class to book it and I am so glad I did because I walked around all day and discovered La Jardin des Plantes. It is so beautiful!

I am taking Susi back for lunch.

This morning, we also had a walking tour of the Marais. The tour was fabulous and the area was very chic and very historic. We went into an old church and I lit a candle for my family. We also saw all the places where Henri IV and Louis XIV lived. It was quite interesting.

Brussels this Weekend!

25/10/97

Wrong, no Brussels this weekend. On Friday morning, we had a class at 9 A.M. at Le Lourve. Our teacher is the airy, artsy type so she was throwing tons of ideas here and there-hard to follow and two hours of standing on hard tile killed my back.

After class we (the girls and I) went to try and book our tickets for Belgium thinking they would only be $20 each way. Fat chance, they were $90 each way. It was a no can do b/c I spent a lot of money in Switzerland. I was tired anyway. When I got home I was trying to take a nap and Madame came in with a package for me from Liv. It totally made my day, b/c I was tired and cussing Paris.

Marianne called and Madame said she could come over for dinner. When she got here Madame had totally set up the kitchen table with a cover, napkins, and a bottle of wine and a full place setting. What a babe! It was extremely nice. TV then bed.

28/10/97

This weekend was fun and crazy! On Saturday, Marianne and I met to go shopping for her birthday which was this weekend. Initially, we met at the Louvre, so we decided to go and look at some art. We headed straight for the Mona Lisa, which was surprisingly small. There was such a huge crowd around it. It was totally not worth it. I don't see what all of the fuss is about!

After we were finished, we headed for the Marias (Me St. Paul). There are tons of fun places to shop and some very trendy places to eat. I went home at 5:00 to get ready for the evening.

Marianne and I went to Justine's house and had champagne, cheese, and persimmons. Justine and Abi had a chocolate mousse with 21 trick candles in it. Except we didn't know they were trick candles. I guess that got lost in the translation. I lit the thing and we had an inferno-couldn't get it out b/c of the trick candles. Finally, I turned it over and threw it out the window. Just imagine four girls throwing a chocolate mousse out the window. Absolutely hysterical! Justine's house is made in the two-story fashion so the cake was still on the first floor roof because Justine's room is on the second floor. It was still on fire on the roof of the first floor so we doused it with champagne. It was a close call but in the same regard very, very funny.

After that, we met Celine (Madame's granddaughter), Ameille, Maude, and Adeline (all three were Celine's friend) for dinner. We ate at a little Italian place near Me: Mabilo -it was good but it was so late by the time we got our food- 10:00. It was Marianne's b-day weekend, so we got a dessert for her with candles etc.

After dinner, we went to the Frog and the Princess- fun. Had a few drinks there and then we went to the Barfly's bar on Champs Elysee. It was expensive, fun and bustling with lots of chic people. This guy named Senny was there and said he liked my physique! It was so funny. He was a banker from Paris but originally from Senegal. He told us to go to Le Bash afterwards. I was like, "Oh, yeah, I'll be there!" but I really wasn't going to go. But after we were so rudely rejected from the Caberet, we went across the street to Le Bash. They wanted us to pay some absurd amount of money so we decided to leave. As we were leaving we saw Senny and he told us to follow him. We went right to the front of the line and got in free. It was great! He bought us all drinks and we danced until 3:30. Lots of fun.

When we left, Marianne and I couldn't get a taxi so we decided to accept a ride from these Parisienne bankers. They took us to their car (a BMW w/leather seats and an awesome sound system.) Too bad they started badgering us and saying we didn't have to go home and to party with them. etc. When we asked to get out they were like, "In a minute." I started to make noise and the people on the street heard us so the guys let us out. It was scary. We decided to take a taxi after that.

Of course, I had 0 money left from the 350 francs that I brought. So angry-kicking myself! But then again, I am never going to live in Paris again so I had better make this memorable!

Got home, I went directly to bed and woke up at 11:30 the next morning when Dave called me. We decided to meet at 2:00 at Le Louvre. It was such a beautiful day! We walked along the Seine and down to the Saint Germain des Pres. Great stores! We had coffee at a trendy place near les Deux Magots. It was a good day.

That night we had dinner at a really, really good Spanish place called L'Escunrae on Saint Germain off the Me Rue Le Bac. We were so hungry and again it was like 10:00 before we got our dinner. I was so tired when I got home so I crashed but Liv called me at 3:30 A.M. and after I couldn't get back to sleep.

Yesterday was another nice day but I had phonetics-yuck. The opera at 7:30. I am so excited. The girls met before to get a drink and then saw Turnadot. It was beautiful! Again, I was very tired.

Got home and went to bed and skipped class today because my leg hurt. Good excuse, right?

11/1/97
White Rabbit!
Susi came to Paris last Weds and it has been a jam packed week full of fun. The first night we had a great dinner at an Indian place off of the Me Strausbourg St. Dennis in the passage Brady. I had a samosa, vegetable curry, and Naan. It was truly fabulous.

After dinner, they gave us this terrible shot on the house! ugh! After we went to the Frog and the Princess for a few drinks. Nathan (he goes to UCSD and he is in my Cours Pratique) met us there and after a while we began to talk to some French guys.

Susi made friends with Sean McGinness with the beautiful long red hair-yes, it was a guy. He was drunk as a skunk with a hostel shirt on, "Young and Happy." He said he was a regular at the hostel Susi was staying in! Great! Later we saw him at another bar and he started to cuss me out when I asked him not to say fuck to Susi.

The next morning we met at Les Deux Magots for petit dejeuner (breakfast). The coffee was really good but the pains au raisen were a little small.

After that, I had to go to class and, Susi went to the Louvre after we met for a sushi lunch by my cours practique class. I ended up skipping phonetics so Susi and I could walk around. We went to Le Bon Marche and the area around the Hotel Lindberg. It is so cute with lots of great boucheries and things like that. All day we walked everywhere and we were exhausted, but we went out to dinner at 8:00. Maude and Celine came with us and we went to a little café right off the Me Palais Royale-Louvre. It was very delicious. We all had salmon which was cooked perfectly. The waiter kept breaking into the rendition of "Tea for Two." That was funny! He had a crush on Susi.

Later, we went to the Buddha Bar and had a few drinks. It was so much fun! We met some French guys. One was a lawyer named Christophe. Very cute and he gave me his number and I gave him mine-which I think was the wrong one. Oh well! C'est la vie!

We saw Abi and Mark, her friend from SF, there and they told us to meet them at Barfly. When we got there I saw two men that I had met at Le Bash last week. It was so weird going into a place and seeing people you know. And.... M C Solar was there- huge, enormous. I was freaking out! He is a huge, French rap guy. There was also another famous singer there named Biba something. But I didn't know.

It was an incredibly fun night. Susi, Celine, Maude, and I had a fabulous time. The taxi driver gave us chocolate and asked us for a kiss on the cheek for means of payment! We pecked away, come on, this was a free taxi ride!

The next morning I had to be up at 9:00 to have breakfast with Dr. Stroup and his wife, some friends from Yuba City. They were coming through town on a wine tour and I was basically going out to breakfast with them to satisfy my dad. They were staying at a ritzy place at the Saint German des Pres. At the end of breakfast, they gave me a silk scarf for a gift. They were very generous and breakfast was delicious.

Yesterday was Halloween- Disneyland Paris...a few thoughts.

1.Clean
2.Fun
3.Freezing, bitter cold
4.Exhaustion

Today Susi and I are on our way to Dijon! Yea!

2/11/98

Susi and I went to Dijon yesterday. It was very cold. We arrived at about 12:00 had a long lunch of salads and coffee.

In the town, there was a hostel where we had reservations but we decided to ditch it and go to a little hotel called Hotel Monchapet. It was very inexpensive and clean. Susi and I checked in and then we went to a big garden/park in the town center-quite picturesque. We finally found the centre ville at around 5:00, which was a really nice area. It was a bummer but lots of stores and banks (I couldn't get $). They were closed because of Tous Saint (All Saint's Day) so we couldn't go to the Grey Poupon factory. ☹ I bought cheap mustard.

Then Susi and I went to a bar and had a drink, a drink, a drink. We ended up getting quite drunk. I was so exhausted & tired (partially from the alcohol) that I felt like shit so we decided to have dinner. Really good. Dijon wasn't full of tourists and not everyone spoke English. I liked it.

<u>Memorable Moments from Dijon</u>
The Center Park
Cartoon Bar
Mustard Shopping
Dropping Mustard off 2nd Floor at Dinner
Arnauld- brat or babe?
Susi's 5 Profound Thoughts
-20 F for Barnes and Noble
-Are those guys gay?
-How much is this dinner going to cost?
-I need more mustard!
-I think I used the men's room!
<u>Irish Whiskies</u> or- what really were they?
Planning Christmas Time
A great friendship!

03/11/97
Tonight we saw <u>Stomp</u>. It was so awesome! It is a musical concert except that the instruments were everyday objects like toilet plungers, newspapers, etc.

After class, I went and hung out with Nathan. It was cool. After I went to AE to change $ and after I walked all around Opera and had coffee at Café de la Paix. I also went to some great stores that had Limoges boxes. They are still rather expensive here.

Tonight coming home on the metro there was this funny drunk man who was singing at the top of his lungs. Abi, Marianne, and I had to pinch ourselves to keep from laughing. It was hilarious.

Right now I'm rather angry because all my apples are gone and so is by Tabooli that I bought the other day -Argh- it's probably the spurned Isabelle._____

11/5/97

It wasn't Isabelle; it was Amelie and Celine who took my food. That's okay. Celine invited me to Bordeaux this summer with her family. Yeah!

Today we had sushi for lunch again. It is so good! And I went to AIFS and got a letter from Ravi, a friend from home. It was kind of random but it was nice to hear from her.

This morning I got three calls, Mom, Liv, and Dr. Juan. I miss Liv so much! Mom was really tired and she said Dad had another sinus infection. Ewwww!

Juan wants to meet me in Prague. On verra! Cooking class tonight!

8/11/97

Thursday night – wow!

Chain of events

Met Abi at 6:00

Snuck into American University

Drank Cider Beer

Went to St. Michel

Dinner and drinks with AIFS

Buddha Bar with Ashby and Abi

Met 4 nice guys- Oliver, JC, Eric?

Bought us yummy drinks all night

Dinner with them next Thursday

Friday morning, woke up feeling very excited about going to Florence and seeing Susi, but also a little under the weather. I was riding with Nathan but he wasn't there yet. As I boarded my train they informed us there was an Italian train strike and that we would have to transfer at the border. I needed water, apple juice, and diet coke so I went off to find them and I kind of ignored the announcement. Nate barely made it on the train but we finally got under way. We met a very nice French girl who happens to live right by me. Her name was Gaille- extremely polite and a tad of a thesbian (actress)-not lesbian.

We are going to see her perform.

When we hit the Italian border hell began. They herded us like cattle into a bus and we took off through the Dolomites. Our Italian tour guide might have been informative if he spoke any other language than Italian and the movie might have been interesting if it wasn't in Italian. The little brat behind me might have been cute if he had not been kicking the back of my seat and if I didn't have a hangover. Let me tell you, nothing good will come from alcohol. But I did have six hours all to myself to think, think, think...

In Milan, we caught a train that ended up being delayed for an hour but finally arrived in Firenze (after a few false alarms and a troubled sleep) at 3 A.M..

Poor Susi had gone to the station at 9:45 to get my ass but I think I was destined not to arrive on time! Nate and I, through sign language, finally got a hotel, slept, and called Susi in the morning.

Nate was going to spend a few days with us in Florence, and then going on to meet a friend in Padua. Susi and I met and walked around and unsuccessfully tried to get a return reservation home.

We ate a good lunch of a white, light wine and a fun rice dish with shrimp and asparagus. Susi told me that she had a surprise-tickets to the opera. I was ecstatic! Anyway, we got all dressed up to go to the opera but before, we went to a wine bar and had a rushed yet fantastically good glass of Chianti Classico. I think I have a new luv (no, not a boy)-Chianti. Nate tagged along for the whole thing and ate dinner with us. After we walked towards the opera and went to <u>Bucca Ognissanti</u> for dinner. I had pasta with mushrooms and a great Bruschetta- It was sooo good- definitely would go back.

We rushed to the opera and luved it depite the fact that we thought it was over after the second act! Nate finally left us so Susi and I decided to celebrate and get a few drinks.

We went to a bar called Capuici and met Vanessa, Fabio, and Marcus. They were fun Italians and they invited us for dinner that night (doesn't look like we'll make it). It was fun to communicate through a mix of four languages.

Today, we went to San Ganignano- a small, beautiful town in the Tuscan hills. The bus ride from Florence took one and a half hours and was very twisty. It was a small price to pay for the beautiful views and the town itself- an ancient castle-like town nestled in the hills. It is known for its boar paraphanelia, i.e., boarheads, plates, and meat. I would luv to take Dad there.

Susi and I ate at a great place (saved receipt). You walked down towards the end where you take a right and the restaurant is on the right side. The food was superb! I got Tuscan vegetable soup and a side of mushrooms and bruschetta to split- fantastic. All day it was either pouring or bright blue. During one of the rainstorms, Susi and I ducked into a leather shop and bought backpacks which we fell in luv with.

After a bus ride back that made me puky car sick, we had sushi for dinner (good but not enough) and gelato for dessert!

"Tomorrow is a new day."

-Jane Kryski

10/11/97

Hotel Constanti is the name of my pensione. It is right off the Duomo. I would definitely return. It is very clean and the patrons are nice. This morning I got up around 8:30. I had a fabulous sleep so I feel much better today. This morning I got up and went to American Express. The woman wasn't quite as bitchy today. Luckily I was able to get reservations back to Paris and a couchette! Yeah! After American Express I went and had a fabulous cappucino at a place called Gilli - it is to the right of the Duomo walking away from my hotel. I must admit that the Italians can make a damn good cappucino- the perfect amount of froth that doesn't have too much milk- it really makes my day!

After that, I went to the Duomo. It is absolutely huge. Very beautiful but hard to see some of the paintings because of the dim lighting. I lit a candle for my family and said a prayer. I am feeling very religious. I then decided to go the Academia but it was closed today because it is a Monday (most things are closed on either Sun. or Mon.).

I kept walking around and found another less crowded church. Smaller with lots of old paintings. Don't exactly know what it was called but it looked important.

After the church, I went and got a petite Italian pastry. I must admit that I have been pleasantly surprised at how good the pastries have been here!

Next, I checked out the Museo dell Opera di San Maria del Fiore. Great museum! I saw the Pieto and the St. Mary Magdalene. I would definitely recommend returning. The admission was only 8.000 L. Not too, too bad!

Gotta go because I have to meet Susi at 12:30.

Later…

Met Susi and we got lunch at a little side café which seemed to be good. After lunch we strolled along the Arno River across the Pont di Vecci. The river was very cute and looks a lot like the Seine.

Susi and I then caught a bus up to a little town called Fiusali- quite beautiful. If I were staying in Firenze I would return at 5:00 to watch the sun go down and then have dinner in one of the cafes overlooking Firenze and other views of Tuscany.

Susi and I enjoyed each other's company over a refreshing Coca light and a Diana cigarette while overlooking all of Firenze. Ahh, life is so sweet!

We then went to her school and then back to her house. I finally met the infamous Giudo and Immanuela (Susi's house-parents). They are a typical Italian couple. Right now it is storming (thunder & lightning) and Immanuela is cooking up a very good-smelling dinner.

Later…

Dinner was so good but there was a lot of it. To start we had risotto with artichokes and asparagus. So, so good. Dinner was salad, squash, chicken, and a fruit salad with gelato to finish.

The language barrier wasn't that big of a problem because I understood nuances of Italian and because Guido spoke French. They kept teasing Susi and me because Marco and Fabio had called four times for us! The grandma was also there and she was hilarious. She kept saying the funniest things and she told Susi she was going to come dancing with us!

Later, Susi and I went to Gilli (again) and had spumante which is like a kir-delicious!

11/11/97

This morning, I went to the Academia to see David, the slaves, etc. It was quite interesting. Probably one of my favorite museums so far. I stayed there for an hour and 45 minutes and then got a Coca Light and read on the steps of the Duomo until I had to meet Susi.

We had a gelato for lunch and then went to a market and bought grapes and bread. I also bought a few apples for the train tonight.

We then took a long walk on her way home to retrieve some of my stuff from her house. We are going to a Mexican bar in a little bit to get margaritas and chips and salsa.

<u>Top Ten Italian Memories</u>
1) Train strike ☹
2) New Black Purse that I got at the market
3) Opera
4) Marcus, Fabio, Vanessa
5) San Gimingano
6) Lunch in San Gimingano
7) Duel backpack purchases
8) Sushi dinner- only Americans- lots of staring
9) Fiosole- view, view, view
Diana's & Diet Cokes (ok-maybe more than 10)
Dinner w/ Guido & Immanuela
Reading on the steps of the Duomo
Pont di Vecchi

Drinks- wild, fruity & exotic at Gilli
Cappucinos- best in Italia
Oops, that was more than ten.

14/11/97
In class with a big, stinky substitute bitch. She hates me.
Ride home from Italy...terrible...three fat men who snored the whole night. They stunk too.

Wednesday night- cooking class. We made beet salads, chocolate cake, sautéed pears, chicken, mash potatoes, and beans. So, so good.

I miss Liv & Tif & my mom & dad. Tif, who is a good friend from Davis, called this morning and she was really upset. School had her down but it was really nice talking with her. I think we are going on Supermarket Sweep together!

Last night, I went to the Buddha Bar. We met J.C., Olivier, Stephen, and Frederick. They bought us drinks all night and food from the bar. One of the bills was over $400! It was pretty fun. The French guys are bizarre. This one, Eric, asked me if I wanted to go to Italy with him today. I didn't understand at first and then when I finally did I was shocked. This guy is the only one I don't like- he is a total sleaze. I do think Jean Charles is hot. We are taking dinner with him tonight at 11:00 and we are going to meet Nate before for drinks.

Gaille called-sooo nice. Nate and I are meeting for lunch tomorrow (Sat.).

Later...

I just got back from the Buddha Bar (again). Ashby and I had dinner together. It was so good but the portions were huge too. It turns out that Jean Charles called me and said he couldn't make dinner tonight because he had a "reunion" that he forgot about. I was thinking "whatever" until he asked me if I wanted to have lunch with him. Yes, yes, yes...he is such a hottie!

"Time is too slow for those who wait,
too swift for those who fear,

too long for those who grieve,
too short for those who rejoice,
but for those who love,
time is eternity."
Anon.
(read at Diana's funeral service by Lady Jane Fellows)

15/11/97
I pulled my journal out of my bag this morning and Susi had put the little postcard in the back. So cute.

15/11/97
Last night I had dinner at the Buddha Bar with Ashby. It was a very nice time. I ordered two entrées instead of two plats because it cost less $. It turns out that it was more than enough-like I said, the portions are huge. I ordered the Chinese chicken salad and egg rolls. The service took a while so they gave us a plat for free which was very expensive. Afterwards Ashby & I had a disappointing bicarde cocktail (wasn't made right) and then we took Le Metropolitin (the metro) home.

This morning I got up and was feeling not very good. I caught a cold after Italy and it traveled to my throat. I ended up meeting Gaille and Stephanie, Gaille's friend, for lunch-Nate couldn't make it. We went to a fun café on Rue St. Jacques-Fossieres. It was exotic food (great) and the inside was decorated like a rainforest! I had a salade Bresilienne- tasty.

This morning I got a package from my mom- a bundle of People magazine. I was so happy. I had café and read one of them. Apres, I came home and snuggled in bed with another one. Guess who called? Yes, yes- Jean Charles.

We are going to lunch tomorrow at 12:30 at a restaurant called Le Comptior on 37 rue Berger. I'm kind of nervous. I haven't been on a vrai rendez-vous since Septembre. What to wear!

It's Chuckie & Pammie's birthday today and there is a big party which I am missing. ☺ I didn't feel well today so I told Celine I couldn't come to her house tonight. I feel bad because

I think she was disappointed. We decided that we are going out next week. A demain!

16/11/97

Today, I got up at 9:00 after a nice 12 hour sleep. I feel much better! I also went to the Marche au Pleine Air. I bought a mango, grapes, tabuli, pate, and a beet. After, I got ready for my lunch date. I wore tan billowy pants and my brown shirt with flowers- tres drole!

I met Jean-Charles at Le Comptoir at 12:30. I got there early so I had a glass of champagne. You know, for nerves! He is very nice and cute and he speaks perfect anglais. I had poached salmon and tiramasu and another glass of champagne. C'etait bon! Apres, we walked around Le Louvre and then I went into the Louvre after we said our goodbyes. We are going to Buddha Bar again on Weds. Night- barflies we are!

Got off a few metros early to walk home. It's not cold but kind of misty.

When I got home Madame's son and daughter-in law were there with their two kids. Gregoire et Clemence- so cute. They luved me because I gave them candy, curled their hair-even the little boy, etc. They luved Halloween so I taught them how to Trick or Treat. The family invited me to dinner at their house because they live near Versailles.

I really don't want to leave I am beginning to feel like I really fit in. I have Parisienne friends and I really am happy.

Tonight, Celine, Ashby, and I are going to Le Bar Romain. Later...

Too bad we couldn't find the shitty Bar Romain. It was totally unheard of. So I suggested we head into the little unpretentious café where we could get a cheap cocktail. Wrong again.

Jane leads the whole group into the Hotel Concord to order the most expensive drinks we had ever had. They were good but $20.

Later we headed to Barflies and were able to sit down. Nice, nice, nice.

17/11/97

Right now I'm sitting at Café de la Paix enjoying a Coca Light. This morning I called Chuck and wished him happy birthday. He was so tired because he was on his pledge retreat this weekend. He told me the funniest things that he had to do! He also said that they serenaded mom and handed her a rose. She had a smile from ear to ear- that cat, she luved it!

After class I went to American Express and then tried to find the Bar Romain-again. Too bad it wasn't there- only a building under construction. What a scam- I'm throwing that guidebook away!

Dr. Juan hasn't called me since last Weds. Maybe he is losing interest. I was going to tell him not to come to Europe just to see me. I was going instead to tell him that I would prefer to go out in San Fran- hoping maybe that I could somehow fanagle a ticket to the Black and White Ball. That would be fun, now, wouldn't it! I know, though, that in March Aunt Pammie might need me to help with her gala event and the Taylors', the people I work for at home, might need me to help with their Farmer's Market. I also have skiing and aerobics on top of that so I should be fairly busy.

Café de la Paix is such the place to be seen. There are all of these people in here trying to look like they are someone with their phones ringing every two minutes. Comical! I am excited because by parents are probably coming to Paris in Feb. Yeah!

Scoop...

Jean-Charles is a top executive in France Telecom and he is 32. Geez. Olivier owns four jewelry stores. They are both loaded. Everyone (on AIFS) is so jealous because I have met so many French people and am hanging out with them. Nah! Nah!

Places to go... Belgium/ Brussels

After finals...

Interlaken- couple days; skiing

Rome and Venice- sight seeing; couple days Dolimites-

skiing; couple days
> Val D'Asaire- skiing; couple days
> Salzburg, Vienna- skiing; couple days
> Prague- sight seeing; couple days
> Poland?? / Germany??
> Feb. 18th Mom & Dad.

19/11/97

On Monday night, I finally got a call from Tanya. I think I will be going to Rennes on the weekend of Nov. 28, 29, 30. She is so weird on the telephone- always stuttering and what not. She asked me if Karinne had called me yet and when I told her no she said that Karinne has been thinking of calling me. How thoughtful! I have a cousin in Paris and she has been thinking of calling me. What a great girl! The damn pain in the ass.

Yesterday, I met Celine for lunch and we went to my favorite Japanese place. It was good. Later, we went home and did homework while listening to music.

I had the ballet at the old opera last night. It was so beautiful. Ashby and I met before at the Café de la Paix to have a drink. I'm decidedly sticking to salads now because I feel pudgyness coming on, detest that!

Tonight- cooking class and then Buddha Bar.

I called Liv this morning and we had a long talk. We laughed so much! I'm very excited about seeing her at Christmas and going home! I'll be home for good on March 1st. Then I can start aerobics to get ready for Mexico, where I am going on my next trip! Yeah! Yeah! I haven't told my dad yet. Do you think he'll be mad?

20/11/97

Twenty five days until I go home for X-mas! I can't believe that. Last night we had cooking class. Oh, it was so good. We had two legs of lamb, baked in the oven with patates, beans in tomato sauce, moules in a white wine sauce, and to finish it was a Tart Tartin- probably the best dessert I've had so far.

After that Abi, Ashby, and I went to the Buddha Bar and had some drinks with Jean-Charles, Olivier, Eric, etc, and some French girls. It was fun as usual and we're heading back next week but also Jean-Charles asked if we could get together before that. Why not?

Liv called me this morning-at three. I'm so glad my friends have such strong faith in our relationship! They can call at any time of the night- which they seem to have done quite a lot lately! No, I luv hearing from them. I'm so glad I have faithful friends because so many people here are bummed that they haven't heard from their buds.

Just remembered…(with my guelle de bois- hangover). Last night I met this really nice Parisienne, girl but Jean - Charles and I made up this total lie saying I ran away from home and then we eloped and I'm going home for Christmas to see my family for the first time in six months. Such a huge fat lie. So, of course, she wants to have lunch with me on Monday! What do I do?

Later the next morning…

It's 10:45 and I'm sitting in one of my favorite haunts-Café de Cluny. I walked to school today. A very nice walk. I think I'm going to start doing that more often. It took 45 min. at a good power walking pace. It was very easy…

L onto Rue Grimaldi

L on Rue Sevres @ Metro Sevre-Lecoube

Continue on Rue du Four

R on St Germain des Pres

Only problem is that I went past so many fun stores. I had to stop five times because I saw so many cute shoes! I think I'm going to walk to Le Louvre tomorrow morning.

Groove on Michael Jackson-"you are not alone".

P.S. I don't think I have ever been so happy!

21/11/97

Today is very cold. I luv it! I'm wearing my peacoat, white ribbed turtleneck, gloves, and my beanie. I look so chic!

After art today, I couldn't quite make it to Cours Pratique so I went on a Bateaux Mouche ride. I took the Me Alma Marcel. When I got off there was a memorial to Diana-I was so sad! But I did luv the Bateaux Mouche. Right now I'm having some tea to warm up!

24/11/97

On Friday night, Ashby and I went to Au bon Couscous- it was bon and I had couscous-big surprise! Afterwards, we met Gaille and Stephanie and Nate. We went to a little café and tasted the Beaujolais Nouveau. Ashby said she didn't feel well so we left.

She is awesome but when we are in a big group she can get weird. When we got in the taxi she said she felt better and wanted to get a glass of wine at the Hotel de Crillon. It was so expensive but she paid the bill so it was OK.

That night or, I should say morning Dada called me (at about 2:00) and we talked for half hour. I am very excited about them coming in Feb. I think that we are going to Normandie. That is going to be great because by then I will have seen most of the regions of France.

On Sat. Celine and I went to Champagne. We took the train to Reims and then had lunch at a little bistro. We were able to get in on the tail end of a tour at Tattinger and then buy some champagne. When we got back to Paris we went to her house and had dinner (salmon).

After dinner I presented a half bottle of champagne to her mother. The right thing to do because she luved champagne-her drink of choice. We watched Casino and did nothing all day Sunday. It was so nice. I had to study Sunday night because I had a midterm in Societe Francaise.

Got up this morning (early) to study and then walked to school which took me 45 minutes. Test was long but really not too bad.

It is colder than a well digger's ass-freezing. Brrr!

25/11/97

Last night, we went to a fun bar called Lizard Lounge. It was off theMe St. Paul-Marais. I had the best gin fizz I've ever had (I actually don't think I've had one before-so it had better be my best). Quite good! My back is really hurting though-maybe my bed?

Today, I had lunch with Gillian, an AIFS girl from New York. Lindsay called her a JAP-a term I had never heard before. I, personally, think there is nothing wrong with being a Jewish American Princess. If I were Jewish, I think I would be labeled one. I am a Daddy's Girl to the extreme. Anyway, I kind of like Gillian. I think we are going to travel together from Jan21-Feb.2.

So far we have an itinerary. We are going to start in Suisse. Ski for a few days and then go to Poland for two days. Then off to Italy-Rome, Florence and Sienna. She is then going back to school and I am going to ski in the Dolimites and meet her in Val D'Asar the next weekend to ski some more. Then I'm going up to Salzburg and Belgium-ski. Afterward I'm going to meet Dave in Venice for Carnival!

27/11/97

Flash News-I quit smoking (for 14 hrs. now), Jean Charles and Kirk, a good friend from Davis, called me last night on the machine. Jean Charles wanted me to go to Buddha Bar. Called him and he answered on his cellular and I think I heard some girls whispering in his ear.

Anyway, Kirk's message was cute-miss him tons.

We had dinner at AIFS for Thanksgiving. It was great-ate too much!

I'm going to Tanya's today and I have a Louvre test. Double whammy.

Later...

The test was cancelled because our teacher's son is sick. Actually, she was so frazzled that she forgot our images on the metro. So now we have to take home a test. Ohh, too bad. We discussed our test over a beer before my departure for Rennes.

I talked to Ashby today and she was angry at Olivier because he called Ashby's man (Paul) "Garcon" the whole evening that they went out. Paul was visiting. I knew it would be bad news if she brought them to meet. Anyway, she's coming with me to London next weekend. We are going to Kensington Palace, a theatre and to visit Jackie, my mom's friend and her family- David and Morgan.

Called home this morning and the whole gang was in Yuba just finishing up Thanksgiving dinner. They had stuffing-I didn't. Oh well.

Only had one Pappy (cigarette)-good girl. Didn't even really want one. Screw everyone who said I was addicted.

30/11/97
RENNES-BON WEEKEND
Oh Mon Dieu! Please, no more Thanksgiving dinners. I honestly can't move!

I went to Rennes this weekend and it was absolutely formidable (terrific). I was so wrong about the Fremaux family. They were so nice and accommodating. I was pleasantly surprised. On Saturday morning, I got up and met Remy, my 25-year old male cousin, who had arrived later than I on Friday night. He was sleeping in the same room as Francoise, his finance (too bad because he was hot).

Very shocking considering how religious Nora is.

I guess Tanya and Michel (her husband) are more liberal –they are wild birds! Anyway, Francoise is a big dork-not intentionally-just her mannerisms etc. I don't know why Remy picked her because he is pretty cute. Anyway, Michel is totally cool too. He took me on a tour of the house and his gardens and showed me his cave and his wine relics.

On Friday night he showed me his digestif collection and was so excited that I knew the difference between armangac and cognac. He started pouring little shots for me. He also heard that I liked cherries preserved in alcohol. So he gave me some of them too! He said it would help me sleep better!

Saturday morning, Michel and Remy took me to the marche (huge) and we bought all the makings for a true Bretanique lunch-huitres, boulot, langushiens, fromage, galette, jambon, salad, et fruits. They were so proud of Rennes and the marche. They explained and showed me it all and made sure I got to taste everything. When lunch finished (around 4:00) we took a ride into the country with Claire, Remy's 18-year old sister. They showed me the canal (les eclous), churches, catherals, Les Iffs (the place where Karinne might get married), and some fountains.

What was incredible was that they knew the history and century of everything. We came home and at 8:30 we had soup, a petit quiche, a petit seafood salade, and chestnuts (champignets). All the food was fabulous and Tanya was very concerned that I learn the way to cook it all!

Sunday morning, Tanya and Michel took me to St. Melo to see the ocean. We walked through the city and then to the sea. Since the tide was down we were able to walk out to a petit island where Chateaubriand was buried. The view was fantastique-absolutely incredible. Mom and Dad would luv St. Melo. We also went to the Catherdral de St. Melo, which had beautiful stained glass. It was dedicated to Jacques Cartier who was a Candian and who donated a lot of money to the town. I guess that most of the town was destroyed during WWII and then reconstructed. It was phenomenal.

We got back at around 10:00 and ate an absolutely scrumptious Thanksgiving dinner/lunch. I had stuffing but it was the French style-pretty darn tasty. And there was also wild rice straight from Yuba Duba. Gotta luv it.

And the whole weekend I spoke all French. Only about four sentences in English. I am the woman!

Mom and Dad and I really need to return in February and take them to dinner. It was truly a fun weekend-mais je ne peux pas bouger-trop de manger. Cette semaine je dois avoir une regime.

Also, I bought a bottle of Veuve Cliqoit and brought it to Rennes. Good move-they luved it. We drank it before our Belgium chocolates, after our huge turkey feast, and with our raspberry tarte/mousse cake. Fabulous!

1/12/97
White Rabbit!
Today I tried to walk off my huge Thanksgiving dinner. I had coffee for breakfast and then walked to school. I had to sit through Societe Francaise for two and a half hours and I got a C+ on my midterm. Total bullshit. I was so pissed I didn't have the heart to go to Cours Practique.

So I skipped it and took a walk through the Luxembourg Gardens. It was truly beautiful. I found myself near Me Vavin so I hopped on the metro and took my shoes to the cordinner by Me La Tour Marbourg (where Brad Pitt was spotted last week by Gillian). I bought a sweater at Bennaton and booked two reservations for Madrid- 400F- ouch!

I got home and did homework all night, talked to Liv, and got a call from Dr. Juan who is 38, has a real estate office and an ex-wife who took all of his household items when she left him-oh and I forgot to mention, he has three kids. I was trying my hardest not to burst into giggles on the phone-this guy is way out of my league!

Why are all the older men attracted to me?
It's so COLD here!

2/12/97
Il neige! Comme n'importe quoi! Snowing, snowing, snowing!

3/12/97
Last night we went to Cyrano DeBergerac at a theatre near Me Trocadero. It was a great cast but kind of hard to follow. It started at 8:30 and supposedly lasted until 12:00. Chad, Dave, and I cut out at intermission because it was Shane's birthday. We met him and Virginia, his girlfriend who is studying in

Scotland, at Hard Rock Café to celebrate. I had a Sex on the Beach and two Coronas. The guys are cool but refuse to go to French places because they say the prices are too high, but they'll go to Hard Rock and pay the same price. We started talking about NYU and Dave busts out with "New Yorkers are all a bunch of assholes." And then Shane starts with "I hate the fucking French." It's so funny.

This morning I went to Montmartre w/AIFS and had a café-beautiful. I luv that area! It's so cold!

6/12/97

Well, I'm obviously not in London. I decided not to go after I left my traveler's checks at home and after Ashby couldn't go (she got cut off). I was going to hang out with Chad and Shane but they were basically being punks. They were all hyped to go and then they were all "we are staying with a friend so I don't know what you are going to do." God-damned assholes- I was so pissed. Luckily I was able to change my reservations so I can go at a different time in Jan. and spend more time.

On Weds. Ashby and I went to dinner in the Latin Quarter and then had a drink at the Buddha Bar. Then I was supposed to meet Jean Charles but he was 35 min. late. Luckily I saw my friend Louis and I sat with him for awhile. J.C. finally came but I only stayed for 45 min. because I had to meet Celine, Gaille, and Stephine at the Atmosphere at 11:00. It was fun but we were all tired.

Last night I stayed home and read because I got a new shipment of People magazines. Gotta luv my mom!

Today I'm meeting Dave at 11:30 to do La Defense and then we are going to go shopping. Tonight- Barfly.

7/12/79

Yesterday and last night were so much fun. Grand Arc (La Defense) was okay but after we walked up and down the Champs Elyse I couldn't get a reservations at Barfly so Ashby and I went to the Latin Quarter and had sushi. Afterwards we went to the Barfly and had some drinks. The barman there is so cute! I ran into that awful man from Senegal named Senny. He is degountant (disgusting). He was all over me and basically ruined my time there. Ashby and I got pretty toasty...she is so much fun to party with. We saw our friends Nate, Yvonne, and Cloe there. There we all jived up and were ready to party. Ashby was absolutely lapping me with cocktails. She kept saying "just one more." We eventually got Blue Hawaiis. They were so fun- big cocktail glasses with pineapple and cherries as decoration. But this whole time Senny is touching me everywhere and asking me if I've ever slept with a black guy, etc. He was really offensive. I finally told Ashby that we had to go. We were walking down the Champs Elysee and I was supporting Ashby-very loupy. Then all of a sudden we were like let's go dancing. So we headed to Le Bash. There was a little crowd out front. We were picked right away and told, to come in. We walked in and right pass the cash register . We didn't have to pay a cent-on Saturday night-incroyable! The music was really good. I saw my friend Melissa there and it was her friend's birthday. I guess she was loaded so she had a private table so we were able to go on the upper level. It was fun until Senny showed up-ahhhh-he is so nasty-but filthy rich. He should just buy a slut because he's never going to get someone like me.

Sunday I slept in because I got home at 4:15A.M.. I got up and went to Le Louvre to work on my paper. I sat in the bookstore and copied info out of books for an hour. I was lucky because no one said anything to me and I ended up not having to buy a book. I then went to this store in the Louvre and bought Liv a beautiful, classy, elegant Waterman pen. It was damned cher but she is truly my best friend and I wanted to get something to show her how much I appreciate her correspondence, etc.

Anyway, afterwards I couldn't deal with the metro so I just started walking. I walked one an a half hrs. until I got home. It was really nice. Celine and the gang were there. Celine's dad is buying dad a bottle of wine. He's a cool guy!

Had dinner and got a call from Liv. Private info. She got a hottie man and I have rein. Je suis jaleuse! Lucky girl!

Also Dr. Lopez called. Poor depressed man. He has three kids and he has been married for 13 years. I asked him why he was calling me and he said he didn't know. I told him I had a boyfriend but he still asked if I wanted to see him over Christmas. No! Or if I wanted to go to Australia with him-all expenses paid. NO WAY. I think he is lonely and his life is a wreck. He needs to forget about me because it just isn't going to happen.

Talked with Mom and I am so excited about going home. They are stoked too. We were squealing.

I revised my itinerary. Instead of going to Berlin and Poland it looks like we are going to Chamonix in Savoie and Prague. I also threw Salzburg and Budapest in there instead of the Dolomites. And instead of Val D'Isssere it looks like I am going to stay longer in Chamonix. And if I can't sell my Eurostar ticket I'm going to have to go to London instead of Belgium.

10/12/97

I can't I believe I go home in five days. Incredible. I talked to Kirk. He and Tif are having problems and he is all bummed. I just don't know what to tell him anymore. He knows what he is getting into.

Last night I went to the Bus with my friend Melissa. Very chic. It was girls night so drinks were free and we didn't pay a dime. The door policy is very strict so Melissa and I went first while Abi and Justine went behind us about 5 minutes later. We got in right away but Abi and Justine got rejected. Their dress wasn't right. I felt bad but then again what can you do?

Got home at 3:00 after a harrowing taxi-ride- I have come to the conclusion that all taxi drivers are psycho.

It didn't help that I had class this morning at 9:00. I wanted to walk but it was raining like Hell.

Took a nap and feel better.

12/12/97

I'm having such a moral crisis today. I don't know if I should stay another semester or go home. It's really getting to me. I think I'm going to call Mom.

Last night, Celine and I met Melissa in front of Hotel Crillon so we could go to the Buddha Bar. Guess what! Pierce Brosnan was staying there. We asked these guys because all these stalkarazzi were waiting outside. I didn't actually see him but I felt his presence-it was a peaceful warm feeling!

Buddha Bar was OK. These fat Arabs asked us to dine with them but they were too nasty so the answer was no!

Afterward, we went to the Barfly where I met these really cute French guys and another Canadian who was doing his grad work at Harvard-Hello! He also did undergrad at Princeton. What happened to me along the way?

They were very cool and they wanted our #, etc. to see us again. Pas un probleme! Melissa also met this big hotshot Columbian who we think was into drugs. They invited us to the Bash (luv that place). Of course, they had a private table with private alcohol, etc. We didn't have to pay a dime.

I was dancing and this French guy thinking he was sexy says, "Tu as un grande taille." (You are a big size-I am tall-NOT fat-Hello) Uhhh, screw you! Left that loser pretty quickly.

Had to leave around 2:30 because I had a 9:00 this morning. What was I ever thinking with a 9:00 on Monday and Friday!

Crazy girl!

13/12/97

Ahhh! I'm leaving in two days. I've made up my mind to stay. I just need to talk to Mom and Dad and see what they say. I would really like to get my diplome from the Sorbonne, and I would like to become fluent in French. Plus, I could go to Greece over spring break with Melissa. I'm just so confused!

Last night, I went with Gaille and Stephanie and Nate to see a fabulous film called, Nathan Le Sage. All in French- it was great. Afterward, we went to the Champs Elysee to Chesterfields and then had a Coca Light. It was a pretty mellow night.

Those guys from Barfly called me!

14/12/97

Ahh! I'm leaving tomorrow! Last night was so much damned fun. I'm getting ahead of myself- Celine et moi had lunch in Versailles with Veronique, Bruno, Clemence, et Gregoire. Celine and I got off the RER and were so lost. We walked around Versailles for 30 mins. It's really a beautiful city. When we finally got there it was about 1:00. We found that Veronique was a fabulous cook. We had veal, rice, asparagus, and dried prunes, cake, mousse au chocolate, chocolates, and café. I had very small portions because I learned my lesson from Thanksgiving.

We went home and I studied for a while and then got ready to go to the Barfly for dinner. It was fabulous. I had mushroom salad, six sushi, et fresh pineapple. Not to mention that Ashby and I finished off a bottle of wine. We then went to the Bash. Walked right in again and didn't have to pay a dime. God, that is nice! We saw Olivier there and he bought us drinks. We then saw this guy named Johnny whom we met at the Buddha Bar. He bought us roses, cigarettes, photos, AND we sat at his private table and drank his Johny Walker Blue Label. I think that is expensive! He also offered me cocaine. Thanks, but I'll pass tonight!

So much fun- danced the night away and got home at 6:00 A.M.

Tonight, I had dinner with Chad and Shane near Me Odeon. Absolutly fab! But I'll have to say bye to Ashby, Chad, Shane, Justine, and Marianne tomorrow.

I'm becoming a very emotional person.

15/12/97

Well, I'm on the plane and actually rather pissed. This guy

who checked me in said I was going to sit in 1st class. Now on the plane I am nowhere near 1st class- I'm in economy with every other loon. I asked what happened so they are checking on it.

Nothing happened but the flight is empty so it doesn't matter.

I want seedless grapes!

20/1/98
Long time no write! Ahh, life is so sweet.
Paris
Chicago
San Francisco
Beverly Hills
San Francisco
Paris
Madrid
Paris

Christmas was fabulous but too short. New Year's was fun in Madrid. I went there to visit Caroline, a good college friend and sorority sister. I had a little run in with a bum who poured beer on my head in our couchette. Got back to Paris and had a lot of studying. Hard tests.

Met a French guy, Laurent who took me to Regine's (hottest, <u>most</u> exclusive, private club in Paris). Laurent called me and we went to see L'Assoice du Diable (The Associate of the Devil) in French. Laurent, can we say is a total smooth operator? I was kind of a prude but got together with him nonetheless. He's been calling and asking me out. He wants to go the to Villa Barclay and Buddha tomorrow. We'll see.

Went to Suisse this weekend to ski. Not much snow at all. 2nd day I skied with these ski instructors- Scott and Medby. They rocked me!! Should have gotten together with Medby but again I was a prude. 20/20 hindsight. He might come to Chamonix to ski with me- 2nd chance?

Kirk

Susi

Laurent

… called tonight. They (Susi and Kirk) sound great- luv school!

I want to stay in Paris! I vow I'll be back- maybe for grad school… Oh, yes, I'll be back!

21-1-98

Found out Martha Dwyer's, the head of our program in Paris, husband died. It makes all your boy, travel, school worries seem so miniscule. I feel very bad for her.

I studied all day and met Melissa at Les Deux Magots for coffee. Maybe Greece with Melissa this summer- wouldn't that be fun!

I'm screening calls because I don't want Laurent to call. But I'm torn, what if Medby calls and I don't pick up? What to do?

Talked to Kirk tonight. He's in luv with a great girl named Katy. It's his B-day this weekend- party at Crawdad's. I'm bummed I'm going to miss it.

two days left in Paris. I'm going to cry!

22/1/98

Went out to dinner with Gillian and two of her friends from London last night. We went to Sushi Yaki in the Bastille- very tasty. Afterwards, we hit the Buddha Bar and met up with Melissa. We (or the guys Melissa was with) spent a lot of money. Later, we decided to try the Cabaret. Melissa and I got in (blondes do have more fun) but the others didn't. We stayed for 15 min. It was so private and so ritzy and so French, we left. I'm surprised we even got in.

After, we went across to the Bash- didn't pay of course- and met up with Gil and her two friends. Somehow they got a table at Le Bash and ordered a bottle of whiskey ($250). We were smoking $50 Monte Cristo's- it was a fun night!

1-2-98

So much has happened! I have finally left Paris and not at all happy about that. The last night I met Melissa at Montparnasse to see a movie. The French are such movie freaks. Out of eight theatres we found one movie that wasn't full- My Son. Absolutely terrible! After we went to the Barfly. I met a hot guy from Holland who bought us drinks. I had a great time talking to him- about his wife and three mo. old baby. Later, we went to Le Bash. As I was checking my coat I saw Laurent who had been calling me all week to dine and sleep over at his place- whatever. I told him earlier that night that my grandma was sick and that I might have to fly back to the U.S. Well, he was pretty pissed when he saw me. He came over to me and said, "Tu caches de moi? " (You hide from me)? I said no and he then pinched my cheek and wouldn't let it go. I had a red mark there for about half hour- what an ass!

The music was great at the Bash. We had met a few people earlier who secured a table and bought a bottle. Melissa and I danced the night away. Lots and lots of cute guys were there- of course we danced with them all. One guy asked me to come into his store the next day because he wanted me to model for him. Oh right!

Later, we met up with our French friends Bruno and Marcel and we went to Les Bains Douche. It was 4:30 by then so I went home. The next day I said my goodbyes and met Gillian at the train station. On the train we realized that we were going to La Plagne one day too early. I was so mad at myself because a friend of mine was opening a new disco and invited me to a private party and dinner that night. Tant pis- I missed it. Gil and I stayed at La Palambo in Aime La Plagne. For dinner, we had the woman make up wild bread- it was an ordeal explaining that one. It basically is cooked pizza dough but it is very good

The next day, we headed up to La Plagne Bellecote where we met our psycho roommates in our 1970's ghetto apartement. Marc, Julien, and Samaya were pot-smoking, smelly, dorky slobs. We couldn't stand them. The first night we went to dinner and had great wasabi salads. Later, we saw, Seven Years in Tibet in French. Good flick! After we went to Le Jet- a sorry excuse for a disco. It was a bad dream from the 80s. To combat the total craziness of the situation we started taking shots. That is how we comically became known as the "Filles de Vodka."

After, seven Lemon drops and too many nasty come ons from the Firemen we headed upstairs. The next day began the best week of skiing in my life. Incrediable weather, long slopes, and great chairs to sun ourselves on during lunch. I had a truly fabulous time skiing with Gil- so tiring though. The first night we got a massage- my first. It felt so great! On Weds. we had a crepe fete with our dork roommates. Gil made better crepes than any of them.

After, we went snow mobiling. At 9 P.M. we were freezing but Gil and I were screaming over the slopes. It was great fun. When Gil took over driving we had a little accident and tipped over. Our guide circled around and said in his broken English that we didn't "shift your big bottoms." We informed him that we didn't have big bottoms so he said, "O.K. you didn't shift your little big bottoms." We were freezing after that with snow in our boots and jeans!

Earlier, we saw Souviens toi- L'ete dernier. I Know What You Did Last Summer. It was the scariest movie I have ever seen. Gil and I were shrieking and holding on to each other. Scared the hell out of me. After the movie we were supposed to meet Michel and Guillome (the O.T.U. men) at the Jet. They said they had a bottle of vodka for us- les filles- they were late so we took off. The next day they were bent out of shape but said they wanted a photo of us and them.

their address:
Michel and Guillaume
O.T.U.
Plagne Bellecote
Appart. #171
73210 La Plagne
tel: 04.79.23.40.12

On this trip we were such an entity. There were no pretty girls and everyone luved seeing "the filles." Free drinks and all.

Highlights and Memorable Sayings
*Restaurant 2700m –enorme
*Franchement / C'est clair
*Le Jet
*Skiing on the Glacier
*losing the pudding in the snow
*lunch time chairs
*deck of cards
*leaving the room dirty for the roomies to clean
*snowmobiling
*Haircut and massage
*O.T.U. Viyage- Michel and Guillaume
*Salsa and Ruffles
*"Les Filles de Vodka"
*coffee and cigarettes
*Damit de Kornflaken – German cereal boxes

We left Sat. night for Rome. We were tired and hungry. We got on the train and the man was nice enough to give us a couchette with only two beds. We were able to throw all of our luggage on the ground and sleep.

We got into Rome and picked... Youth Hostel Roma Inn Keiko- Bad Idea! What a shady place! First of all, getting there we got ripped off by the taxi driver. The hostess, Melanie, was such a true to life crack head. She asked us seven times to do a "favor" for her. Tell her boss that "Melanie" brought us there from the train station. That way she gets 5,000L more for each person. What a druggie!

Gil and I were starving so we went to lunch. Good stuff! We had vegetable soup and bruscheeta and four glasses of wine between the two of us. The wine was great but proceeded to give us nasty headaches.

We mastered the metro and went to the coliseum and the

ruins. Really pretty. We bought water paintings of Rome and took a carriage ride with a horse named Romeo. On the ride we saw the Capitol, the Musselini, and so much other great stuff. We walked around afterward and then came back for a lengthy nap. For dinner, it was brushetta, wine, gnocchi and gelato. Great day!

I'm not quite sure how I chose to travel with Gillian but she is such an easy going, fun, and daring chick. She is not moody and so easy to get along with. It has been one of the best decisions I've made in Europe.

2-2-98

Today we went to Vatican City. We saw the Sistine Chapel. It was beautiful but smaller than I had originally imagined. We also saw St.Peter's Basillica. That was probably my favorite monument. The church was huge with ornate gold designs. I gave some money and said a prayer for my family. Later, we had lunch. I had a fabulous polenta and Gil and I split bruscetta. The red wine here is the best I've ever had- so smooth and tasty.

After lunch we saw Campo di Fiora, the Pantheon, and St. Maria's Church- the only Gothic one in Rome. We also met an alumnus from my sorority and her husband. They told us to quit smoking because it was going to turn our teeth yellow!

Tonight is my last day of smoking. Tomorrow I meet Dave in Chamonix, and he is NOT a smoker.

I can't believe it's my last day traveling with Gillian. I had such a good time with her. I'm going to meet her and her man at Buddha on Feb. 19th at 10:30. Hopefully, she can meet Mom and Dad and then later we can go to Le Bash.

Ariba Derche Roma!

4/2/98

An odd twist to the story...

I'm in Chamoix with Dave, and who also is here but Medby. Yes, the guy from Switzerland at Balmer's. I was walking down the street with Dave and I saw him. We went out for a few drinks last night and messed around a little. He wants me to stay with him at his hotel on the night of the 6th. I said o.k. but now I'm not so sure because it seems kind of sketch. I was supposed to ski with him today but he didn't show and I left a message at his hotel to come to dinner at Les Pelerins, our hostel, but again a no show I don't know what to do.

I called Liv from the top of some mountain in Chamonix but the connection was bad and I couldn't hear her.

Chamonix is awesome. The town is cute with lots of shops and nightlife. The slopes are incredibly challenging and kind of icy. I was all jello and shaky after only four runs this morning.

I'm staying at Les Pelerins Auberge de Jeuness with Dave. It's a good deal for food and lodging but it is far from the center of Chamonix and they only give you a choice of four out of eight stations to ski at in the Vallee Blanche with the package I'm doing.

Dave is a character. He still claims to have acid renflux, so all he eats is bread. I've seen him eat four baguettes today. His ski ensemble is another thing, all together- wow! It is so mismatched and Americanized.

5-2-98

Today, we skiied Le Brevet which is better than Les Flegers which we skied yesterday. Medby didn't come to dinner last night but he did meet us this morning at 8:45. He was very reserved and he didn't wait for me at lifts, etc. He acted like nothing had happened. I decided to ski only until 1:00 because

I was tired and sick of his act. The slopes were the hardest I've ever done, so at least I could use fatigue as an excuse. When I was leaving he said he was sorry for how he acted the other night and that he didn't mean to come on so strong. I was thinking, "That wasn't so strong, there's been a lot worse." I told him he was a bizarre boy. Anyway, he said that the offer was still open to stay with him and tomorrow we are going to get a drink at Le Bar Chamonix.

I sent Liv a poster today and bought a headband.

Quote from Dave!

"Oh my God, do you realize Mont Blanc is right outside our window!"

7-2-98

Yesterday, I did the most incredible thing. The night before I was sitting around the hostel with this guy Aaron form Montana. He's a total intellectual who is getting his Ph.D. in chemistry. He is also an international ski instructor. He offers to take me and my friend Carine up to Aiguille du Midi. In order to get up there, you must take two cable cars and then have crampons and ropes to scale this ledge which gives way to the Vallee Blanche. I was scared but this was a chance of a lifetime, so I said o.k. We met him at 10:30 A.M. and went up. At the top, I was interviewed by a camera crew- cool huh? We scaled the walkway with crampons on and then put on our skis to start the 22 km descent. On our way down, we stopped to have lunch on some glacial rocks. The scenery was fantastic. When we got to the hard part there were ice rivers, moguls up to my waist and crevices. It was spectacular- words can't really explain it. It took us two hours and fifteen minutes to get down. At the bottom, we went into these incredible ice caves called La Grotte de la Mer de Glace. Neat stuff!

Last night, we (Carine and I) were supposed to meet Medby at 10:00 and Aaron at 7:00. We missed the bus to meet Aaron and had fondue at the hostel instead. As for Medby, I decided not to stay with him. Yesterday, I was supposed to meet him for a drink at 4:00. I walked in with the others all excited to tell him about my experience. He didn't even say hello, let alone ask how my day was. After fifteen minutes I got up and left and went to the post office. He came in and was all "Are we going to go out tonight or what?" I really liked the guy but now I'm thinking he is a spoiled brat. Tant pis! Will I ever find a man?

8-2-98

Wow, did I ever get burned by that ass, Medby! I'm even embarrassed to write about it! It turns out that he has a girlfriend with whom he traveled with for four months- never said a word about her- and that he also wanted my Canadian friend Carine with whom he is now traveling. What a slime ball! I wrote him a letter before he left and was all, "What happened? What's up?" Oh well, I guess you win some and you lose some.

I found out all this info last night when I was partying with these two Canadian guys named Clinton and Brice. We drank wine and then went to the Aussie bar called Wild Walabies. I got my ass grabbed by Brice or someone there. It was so much fun! I wish Liv was here because the guy to girl ratio is 20 to 1. We would rock this town!

I moved out of the hostel and moved in to an apartment for the next week with some friends and acquaintances from Paris. Our new apartment is tiny. Basically, it's a studio for five people. No room at all. I'm with two Mexicans, Sophia and Christina, one Greek girl named Elena, and an Israeli guy named Aviv. They're cool but too clean. They totally cleaned the room before they set out today. But like I said, they are totally cool!

I took a lesson from Aaron today, Good stuff! Afterwards, we went skiing off piste and had a great time. We skied La Grande Montagne today. It was very challenging with a lot of ice. When I was alone I was coming off a mogul and smacked my shin bone. It hurts! After skiing, I went and enjoyed a vin chaud with a clean view of Mont Blanc. It is so beautiful! I never want to leave. It seems like I always say that, but it's truly spectacular. I am loving my trip abroad- I never want it to end!

*********This is really how the journal ends!*********

I was lucky that my four roommates were decisive. Minutes could have meant everything. I was rushed to the hospital, and while I was being rushed they were searching my room for drugs. They thought this was an overdose, boy, were they ever wrong.

Some doctor, I don't know his name, recognized right away at Chamionix that it was not a drug overdose and had me rushed to Geneva, Switzerland. I was unconscious and continued to be so for six more weeks. At Geneva Medical Center, Universite de Geneva, they diagnosed me as having a brain hemorrhage and rushed me in for brain surgery, all before my parents even knew that I was sick. The following is a report from my friends. I didn't even know what was what, but I guess that this one great girl took it upon herself to call my family. Of course, I didn't have my home address and phone number written in my book, so she called my brother who was living in Chico, and going to Chico State University. Chuck, my brother, tried to get a hold of my parents, but they had the two phones unplugged so they couldn't hear. Chico, being an hour from where my parents lived, was not too far to drive, so Chuck jumped in his car and drove to my town. He alerted my parents and started screaming, "Quick, something's happened to Janie! Something bad."

My parents then boarded the first international flight to Geneva so that they could find. They left three kids at home. One in college and two others, my sister and brother went to a family friend's house.

When my parents got to Geneva, they said I didn't even look like myself. Sure, I still had my hair (which I would later lose), but I had an external shunt which was, to say the least, daunting. My parents were staying in a Hotel Adriatic and they said that the helicopter landing pad was right outside their window. So the whole time, they could hear helicopter blades beating the air. My mom said that they were taking in poor souls that had skiing accidents. It is kind of ironic, not kind of but very ironic that I had no collision on the ski slopes but rather something not at all related to skiing.

After about two weeks, my dad had to go home, because he had a family practice to run, so my aunt came over to stay with my mother for the remaining two weeks that I was in Switzerland. I remember my mother and my aunt scoured Geneva looking for hair clips. My mother said that it was so adorable how the nurses did my hair back into braids. I had long blonde hair then and they did it back in two braids so that I looked like Heidi. That is just one of those things that sticks in your memory. After four weeks in Geneva Med. Centr., my mom and my dad decided I should come home. Then I flew into San Francisco, where I went to University of San Francisco. On the plane I had contracted a severe case of meningitis. My dad met us at the airport and he had the welcoming news that I was sick. The doctors at UCSF thought that my shunt was causing it so they took the French shunt out and replaced it with a good old American shunt. My mother said, "Don't touch her hair, she loves her hair." When my mom came back all the hair was gone except for a small square in the back. My mother said to just shave it all, thinking to herself, Jane is going to be so mad when she sees this.

Well, it wasn't the Swiss shunt because the good old American shunt didn't make matters any better. I remember asking my dad later, "Dad, did you think it was all over?"

All he could do was nod.

I eventually got over the meningitis and at that point I started to emerge from my coma. Some might say like a butterfly from a cocoon, but the worse was just beginning.

One time my brother, Chuck, visited me, and he can't stand anything to do with blood and guts. He could not be a doctor or a surgeon, especially not a surgeon. While I was still at UCSF, I did not look at all like myself. My normal 5'11" frame was shrouded with tubes and I had no hair. My head had an external shunt protruding from it, and I was quite pale from loss of blood

72

(because they were taking so many tests). My brother turned green and he asked, "Is that Janie?"

About two weeks after I arrived, I started to emerge from my coma, I don't remember much. I do have one memory though, and I will share it with you. I remember sitting in the foyer with both my parents and my dad had lunch (my dad needs to eat at 12:00). He was eating a tuna salad and some bean salad and a Snapple. I remember thinking, "How rude of him that he is not giving me any of the bean salad!" I would have liked to say that but I couldn't speak for four months, and little did I know that I had a gastrostomy tube in; I didn't have a swallowing reflex so I couldn't have eaten the bean salad anyway.

About a month after I arrived at UCSF, I was transferred up to Sacramento- to Mercy General Hospital, which was only 45 minutes from my house. At Mercy, I started playing this game with myself. I thought I was in another world and what I had lived up to this time was void. I remember thinking that my dad's car would take me home, but on a trailer. I could not speak but I couldn't tell, so it didn't really matter. While at Mercy, I had this nurse, and occupational therapist, and physical therapist- (Teresa, Keri, and Duane, respectively) really believed in me. Duane and Keri worked as a team and Duane would get beads of perspiration on his brow while they were working with me because it entailed so much physical exertion. Teresa cared for me like I was her own daughter, the care that I received there was excellent. My mother came to visit every single day, and my dad as often as he could, which was about three to four times a week. Teresa and my mom would sit up in my room and talk to me, and then Teresa would do stuff, like bathe me and pour liquid food down the gastrostomy tube to nourish me. The gastrostomy tube is a tube sticking into your stomach so that the nurses can feed you. If I hadn't had my parents along with Duane, Teresa, and Keri I don't know what I would have done.

Then my parents decided to send me to Santa Clara Valley

Medical Center because they had heard that they had a good traumatic injury center. Wrong, they have an excellent spinal cord injury center, but their traumatic injury center was, shall we say, lacking.

I lasted for about a month there until I threatened to commit suicide (on my letter board). My parents sent me back to Mercy.

During the time I was at the Valley, my mother stayed down with a friend, Marion Kline, and she visited me when she wasn't at Marion's, which was every day. One time she came to visit and we were sitting in the room and this guy, who was traumatically injured, kicked the chart cart down the hall and the charts went flying. My mother and I jumped in my bed and hid with the covers over our heads. Two people in a little hospital bed. I knew then that, "I had to get the hell out of Dodge." It wasn't that I was scared, but I was three and a half hours from my home and I could tell the whole ordeal was wearing on my mother. See, there was a bunch of gunshot wounds and car accidents; that is where they get the title of traumatic injury center. I had a traumatic brain injury, but it wasn't externally traumatic. This wasn't the place for me and I made sure my parents knew it. They did know it too, but they didn't act on it until I made a commotion.

One day my two brothers and sister drove all the way down to learn how to transfer me. Before you could take me out, they had to learn how to transfer me. So this is why my brothers and sister came down. When they got there, the head of physical therapy just blew them off, and told them there was nobody to teach them how to transfer me. My brothers and sister had to calm my mom down and physically hold her back from socking the head of physical therapy. Needless to say, the hospital found someone to teach them very quickly.

The one bright spot about my stay down there is that I learned to talk again. That was a very good thing, but nobody spoke English down there, so when I had to go to the bathroom, I had to tell them through sign language, (and that was very hard with one hand). Now, I could say "Bathroom!" and most would understand, but it was difficult none-the-less.

I had an empty bed next to me until about the fifteenth day and then I got this older, female roommate. She also did not speak English. One morning, around 2 A.M., I woke up to the ranting and raving of her in her native language. She had what they call Sundowner's Syndrome, where you get really disoriented when the sun goes down. She was hit by a car while she was visiting, and I felt very bad for her, being in a foreign country and in a hospital where she didn't know what was going on. That WAS the situation I was in. Fortunately, I was not in a coma and not awake to partake in it.

My departure from that Hell hole was July 9th and my mom and I were anxiously awaiting that. When the day finally came we got into the car and drove all the way back to Mercy, where my dad was waiting for me with a diet soda. If you know me then you know that I luv diet drinks.

My nightmare was not ending but really was just beginning. At Mercy, which my mom called the Country Club, they (Matt, a physical therapist asst., who was part of my "team," and Duane) had picked out a corner private room with hardwood floors, and it was right down from the showers. It was truly a homecoming, or as close to home as I could get at that particular moment.

At Mercy, they really catered to my needs. I was the youngest person there, and the rest were all old fogies, save one or two. They siphoned off this room for my breakfast, and they let me eat my lunch and dinner in my room too. You, see, I didn't want anything to do with "those people." While there, I got lots of visits, especially from Keri, Duane, and Teresa. Teresa would stop by on her way home from work- she worked on the top floor, and I was now on the bottom floor, the Rehab Floor- and we used to talk and talk.

I was in there about a month before I went home for good, and about this time my family started taking me home on Saturdays and bring me back on Sundays. This was like a taste of the outside world for me, and I wanted more and more freedom. About this time my mother brought Cookie to the hospital. She was going to be my caregiver (or partner in crime). When I first saw her I thought, yes, this will work. When I finally got out of the hospital, she was there to work 9-5, Monday thru Friday, and with her I faced the world. She was truly my confidante, and my personal buddy. As I write this she is here writing it as I dictate. She is here to write it down, because my stroke affected my right side, and I am right handed, so I am learning to write with my left hand right now, and it's a very slow process.

On August 8, 1998, I went to my house for good. I had my stroke in France on February 8, 1998, and in the States on February 9, 1998, so I was getting out of the hospital a full six months to the day after I originally had the arterial venous malformation, and a full month and a half after I learned to talk again. This was probably the most frustrating thing (other than not being able to walk), the voice thing. I had my voice back, but it was slow and dysarthric and my dad couldn't understand me very well. My sister could understand me the best, so I spent more time around my sister than before. We developed a special bond that wasn't broken when she went away to boarding school in San Rafael for her sophomore year in high school. My voice is much better now and people rarely have a problem understanding me. Anyway, I'm off the subject. When I came home, my dad and sister left for a hiking tour (don't ask) for two weeks, so it was left to my mom, Cookie, and me.

We got along fine, really, although we had some bumps. It was unusually hot, those two weeks, and Cookie later told me that she almost quit. I thought, we would have been up shit creek without a paddle without her.

My 21st birthday was drawing near. As a coincidence, I was born on my dad's birthday. He was going to be fifty-four and I was going to be twenty-one. So as a celebration of my birthday and recent discharge from the hospital, my parents rented a room at the poshist restaurant in Davis (which was called Soga's), and invited a good number of my sorority sisters. I had all of them that came to visit my in the hospital. We had a small private dinner before the festivities, and once it turned 7:30, people started arriving. I got a new black gown and black high heels (I was the bell of the ball). It was surely a night to remember. The only complaint that I have is that it got too noisy and, with my weak voice, it was difficult to hear me. Afterwards, before we started home, my closest friends piled in my dad's car and had me open the gifts that they had brought me.

About this time, my mom and Cookie took me to Sacramento to get an MRI, to try to determine if this thing in my brain was really canernous hemengioma or arteral venus malfarmation. After I had gotten done with the MRI, an attendant came and was going to help me off the table. I didn't want any attendant helping me, for fear of them dropping me. So I demanded Cookie about three to five times. The attendant replied, "It's okay, dear, we will get you a cookie in just a second." My parents, Cookie, and I still get a tremendous laugh from this experience. They must have thought I was really coo-coo. That is one of my main gripes about this disability, people aren't really equipped with the knowledge it requires to tell a physical handicap from a mental handicap. If your voice isn't like everyone else's, they assume you have a mental handicap. I want to be sure everybody knows that I have a physical handicap, not at all a mental one.

After the MRI, my mom and dad took me to Sacramento to see Dr. Cully Cobb and he said if it was his daughter, he would just let the malformation be, and never find out whether it was a cavernous hemangioma or arterial venous malformation (which can reoccur). My parents then took me to Stanford for a second opinion. Dr. Steinberg was the physician (brain surgeon), and he said it might be "radiologically occult" malformation, in which case it had a possibility of re-hemor-raging. I did not want that so I decided right then and there to have brain surgery again and to remove this malformation.

The surgery was scheduled for Dec. 1st, ample time before the Christmas holiday, so it wouldn't shroud the season (that is, if it went well). The day ominously approached but I didn't really think about it until the morning, when I thought, this could be the last time I see my parents. I thought, I am going to have brain surgery. The ride over was tense, to say the least. I said my good-byes, then, what if I didn't wake up from this operation. But, I did wake up, my parents were in the room, and they told me it was an arterial venous malformation and it was under a lot of pressure, so it would have burst sooner rather than later and I would have had the problem all over again, undoing all the hard work. That afternoon, I was in the I.C.U. and I was telling my parents how I felt when I threw up. My dad flipped out and my mom started crying, they thought it was the end, but really it was just another bump in the road. I guess a good deal of trauma to the head makes you throw up. I spent one night in the I.C.U. and two nights in the regular hospital and then about six or seven nights in the rehab center downstairs. The rehab center was like one step above hell. My mother had to bribe me to stay there with a chic new black sweater with a faux black fur collar. At first I thought I'm getting this new sweater, but then I thought, no way. The rehab center was so institutionalized, I was eating breakfast with Cookie and now they had me eating in a communal dining room. I swear, it was like a cattle call. Get all the freaks together and see how they make a mess when they are eating. How inhumane! I demanded to my mother that we go home, but Mom said a promise is a promise, and I had accepted the bribe already. The only thing that kept me sane long enough to withstand the inner torture was that there was a really cute intern there and the thought that I might be home for Christmas- one of my mom's and my favorite holidays. When I finally got out of there, I thought it seemed like months, but in actuality, it had only been nine or ten days.

In the month of November I got a little Welsh Corgi puppy that I named Claire Marie. During all this she stayed with my aunt, the same aunt that stayed solidly by my mom's side in Switzerland. They said they had adopted a tough love policy when it came to Clarie Marie, but I heard stories of my cousins getting the camera and taking a roll of film of Clarie Marie. Claire Marie was the cutest puppy and still is a very cute dog- a German Shepard head on pint sized legs. We have a big German Shepard named Greta, and when Claire is around her, she has the mentality of a big dog. They play fight all day long and Claire lunges her little rotund body at Greta. They do this for hours and hours and it is really fun to watch them.

After the surgery and the subsequent stay at the rehab center, I came home, (and so did Claire Marie). After I came home I had a big question mark buzzed in the back of my head. My dad being a family practitioner could take the sutures out. When he did that I saw that they were not at all like normal sutures but rather a staple inserted with a staple gun. It was then that I realized what a traumatic process I had undergone. I couldn't see the buzz mark in the back of my head, so obviously I didn't care what other people saw. I was brought back to a memory of sitting behind this kid in one of my college lecture halls. He had just undergone brain surgery and he had no hair marks on the back of his head. I remember being revolted by his surgery, and I moved because I didn't want to catch what he had, isn't this memory bittersweet?

My friend, Julie, gave me three hats to wear. I am not a hat wearing kind of girl but I was truly grateful, because I was wearing a ski beanie around and it was not at all chic. When I went to physical therapy, everybody wanted to see what kind of scar I had on the back of my head. I thought, wouldn't all this attention be great if I was not sick anymore?

At Mercy I said I had this little made up world. Let me explain. First of all, in a bizarre kind of way, I thought that the flowers that someone had sent me never died. I remember telling my mom and dad about the flowers, and they said I was kind of coo- coo. They didn't say it in a mean sort of way but I knew then that I at one time had the common syndrome of "hospital disorientation." I also thought at Mercy that I kept changing rooms. But in reality I stayed in the same room during my first stay at Mercy.

I think I mentioned this before, but when my parents took me home, I envisioned myself going home in a trailer on a space-road. This is rather hard to explain, but right before I was to go to S.C.V.M.C. I thought I would wake up and this whole nightmare would be over. I did this for a week, I woke up in the morning and the first thought I had was that if I had a thought at all then I was still dreaming and that this was all a nightmare. All in all, I had a very tough time with reality.

The Christmas I came home from the hospital, I got EXTRA SPECIAL presents because I "was sick." Claire Marie herself got three beds. But I had to face another challenge at the end of this Christmas break- going back to school.

In the beginning of January, my mom and I climbed in the car and faced a 45 minute trek to Davis, where my university town is. My mom went back to school with me and she always jokes, to get her second degree, but in reality she just went back to help me. To help or to hinder, that is the question. My gosh, with my mom I knew my school work up and down. I have often thought that if I put as much effort into my schoolwork before the stroke as I do now, I would have been getting a 4.0. Whereas before, I never would have read the author's note and little optional assignments that we always did. I used to scorn students who would sit in the front row and answer all the teacher's questions, but I am that student now. My mom used to nudge me when the teacher asked a question and say, "Go on, answer it."

It was quite embarrassing because A: I didn't want to speak in a room full of 120 students. B: I have a speech impediment that held me back for a while, but not too long.

We were buddy buddy with the teacher, Krystana von Henneberg; my mom would bring her little articles that should have perked her interest. I would roll my eyes. I tell you, I have never known a teacher by their first name. One day in class the teacher had a slide (she was big on slides) and she asked if anybody knew this particular picture. I spontaneously answered "The Delegate", as the other students were frantically looking through their notebooks. The teacher answered me directly, "That's right, Jane." I wanted to die because you shouldn't answer anything in class as that wasn't cool. The teacher should never, never know your name. My mother, who was sitting right next to me, whispered, "You big fat dork." I slumped even further down in my chair.

My tests were different now. I had a hemorrhage on the left side of my mid-brain so subsequently my right side was paralyzed (I was right- handed) and therefore I had a test taker who I dictated the test to. My test taker was also my reader and this entailed him reading all the books from the class (of which there were thirteen). My test taker and reader was named Bill. Bill was about eighty and hard of hearing so I had to literally shout my answers to him. To take the test we were assigned a little room, somewhere other than the building where the remainder of the students took the test, and I was given double time. One of the problems with the condition I have is, when I'm under pressure or when multiple things are going on, it is hard for me to get out what I am trying to say. So double time to take the test was greatly needed, because I was under so much pressure to get a good grade. This one time, Bill and I were taking this test, I burst into tears because I knew the answer, but I couldn't get across to Bill what I was trying to say. Bill didn't really know what to do, but he got me calmed down enough and I ended up getting an A on that test.

That class was in two parts and two quarters and I received credits in this order: B+ and A-. So I did pretty well, considering.

In between the two classes, my mom, dad, and I went to Arizona for a medical conference. They didn't have any handicap suite, so under the ADA (which has opened up a whole new world for me), it says that they have to have a room. So they did a little shuffling and they came up with the executive suite for the same price as a regular suite. My dad acted as if he didn't know a thing but when we got to the room, he handed my mother the key and said, "Go in and take a look." We were astonished, this room had a big living room, big bedroom, and huge bathroom, and a good- sized closet. We were in heaven.

My mother's cousin, Kris and her husband Dave and their two sons Peter and Lars, live in the same town in Arizona that we were visiting. Kris luvs to shop, so everyday she picked up my mom and me up and we shopped, while my dad attended the conference. I made out like a bandit. While shopping I felt bad for my dad so I bought him this odd fish shirt, and did he luv it! That week was, marvelous. We went out to dinner, drove the golf cart and I had a pedicure.   It was fun!

///

May 15th, 2001

Today wasn't so bad-considering. I had my sociology class and I swear the kids in there are brain dead. There are 60+ kids in there and about ten kids are awake including me. That is one thing that I am thankful about my stroke, one of the only things; this ability to approach my studies in a real way of learning. Before, it was always, what sorority function was I going to that night or who is coming over to "study." My stroke has basically left me with no social life. Don't get me wrong; I had one before all of my friends graduated and moved away. That was two years ago and I am finally graduating now, but I have essentially no social life.

And I am going on to get my master's degree and maybe even my Ph.D. in Rehabilitation Counseling. That will add another five years at least. By then, I figure I will know what I want to do or else have so much education that nobody will know what to do with me.

As I sit here and type these memoirs, I am confronted with all of the sounds and smells of spring. Outside my window, there is a mama bird feeding her little birds. I hear the loud sqwack, sqwack and then, after they have been satiated, the contented silence. I hear the flip flop of the diving board as children submerge themselves for one of the first times this season. I hear the car door slam as the father who lives next door comes home to his family after a long day at the office just to do it again tomorrow. I hear the loud bang of a hammer as somebody takes advantage of the longer hours of the day and works outside. Excuse me, I have to go outside. It is too beautiful to stay in and write.

Ok, I'm back. All around me, I hear and see signs of life. Is this really the new "chosen" life? I know it is not. This new life has been given to me. But did I want it? Want it or not, I got it. I have long since given up on religion. Some say that's a consolation but I don't think so. I think if there was a God that he wouldn't have wanted this to have happened. Not to say my life isn't rich as it is. I just think that girls my age should be doing other things than I am.

There goes that bird again.

The accident. I call it an accident because I did not know it was going to happen, therefore an accident. It really threw my life into a tail spin-as expected. But that's all behind me now. I can't change the past-as much as I'd like to.

Today, like I said, was not too bad. What was bad was yesterday. I called the computer guy at campus (754-HELP) because my computer was acting up. I was having some problems with my Internet access so I was wondering if they could help me. Tall order. You would think I was speaking Chinese. I asked the guy a simple question and he asked me if I (and he spoke to me like I was a moron) would like to form my statement in a question and email it to the campus technical center. I politely informed him that was a negative and he said he had to transfer me. Ok, guy, go ahead and transfer me. So now I had to explain my problem to the next guy who was a little better but he still got hung up on. I just got so mad. And I come to find out after one whole hour on the phone that I could have used bettering myself-yeah right- that I was calling Bovine On-line, the UC Davis Internet access but it was not my primary user, AOL, was who I was supposed to be calling. And then we start the whole process over again. Did I just make any sense? Granted it was a long day and I needed a stiff drink after it was all through and I hadn't even gotten any exercise after it was all finished. But it's my pet peave when people get so hung up on my voice-like a voice tells you how much brains a person has. Well, obviously, to some people it does. I just want to shake the people and tell them that it's "O.K." and to just wait on me and don't make a life career out of it. That is so frustrating! That and people talking down to you just because you have a disability and they automatically think that there is something wrong with your head. I think that is even more frustrating.

\\

Today, I went to the elementary school. Every week I go there And it is like I am seeing the kids anew. They come up with the craziest things to say or ask as a question. Today, we had a play to read outside; the class was split into three groups of eight. I thought, no problem. But, of course, I was wrong. Laura, my cousin, whom I have come to adore and is the school teacher, gave me and my group a play with the instructions to read the little ditty among the students. At this school the kids are rather bright and I must say there are too many Chiefs and not enough Indians. Right away, this little girl, who is actually my pet, took it upon herself to delegate orders. I decided to let her have her time in the spotlight and just sat back and watched until the boys started goofing off. Then, I had to regulate. But it was as if I had an invisible screen on; they didn't seem to hear me. I finally had to scream and they all stopped dead in their tracks. It wasn't just any old scream. It was a blood curdling scream-or as close to blood curdling as I get. But that really got their attention.

There is that darn bird again. Now, it's starting to get annoying.

But anyway, that's kids for you. I am always extra aware of my disability because they always seem to stare whereas adults try their hardest not to look at you. Actually, I don't know what is worse. Now that I think of it. Good job! But with adults it's as if you have some sort of disease they can catch if they look at you. I guess I would rather have that than people staring at you all of the time. The kids were really great when I first came to the class. I was really anxious because I equated kids with staring and I thought, at the time, that was all that I needed. A group of staring kids. But when I got there I was proven wrong. On the contrary, the kids were really, really well adjusted and curious. They were not at all put off by the chair. I now have three "pets" and only three more classes left until the end of the year. Will I miss them? Yes, I think so. Above all of their rowdiness I will miss the little buggers.

Last night was my sister's graduation from high school. It

was really quite unlike mine. I graduated from the high school in Yuba City and it was a cattle call if there ever was one. It was close to 600 kids outside on the football field. Among the spectators, there was aunts, uncles, grandmas, grandpas, mothers, fathers, sisters, brothers, cousins, 4th cousins once removed, dogs, neighbors, and anyone else passing by. It was a cattle call. And what's even more disturbing-yes, I use the word disturbing, when the diplomas were given, in order to be heard above the dim roar, the various spectators would give off a blast with their blow horns. It was quite touching.

At Karin's graduation, which was held in a cathedral, there was no robust burst of noise when she received her diploma. On the contrary, the nuns (and yes, there are nuns) discouraged it; there was an orderly progression to receive the diplomas and then afterwards there was a touching rose ceremony. One of the only good things that came from my hemorrhage (the other I mentioned earlier) was that my sister could live down in Davis with me and commute to Sacramento and attend an all girls, private, Catholic school. Just the way we like them. Oh, and I forgot to mention that they wear uniforms.

There was only one downside to the whole graduation. They had reserved seating and, of course, I was sitting in them. In the front row to be exact. And I was like, "Oh, Hell, ya!" until they positioned a cameraman in front of me. I don't think you quite understand-it was right in front of me. They had a place for "wheelchairs" but I didn't want to have any part of that. When I looked over at them (there were about five) they all had sweat suits on and there was nobody under the age of fifty plus a good majority of them had on bibs. I thanked the good Lord (even though I don't believe in him) for my sense of style and I didn't complain about getting stuck behind the video man. I mean, it's criminal the way that they stick all of the wheelchairs together like they have some God forsaken disease. I guess the people in the wheelchairs don't make it easy for the bulk of the population to think good and willful thoughts about them. What I am trying to say-and I can say this because I am in a wheelchair too-is, in my opinion, that the people who use wheelchairs are at the bottom of the barrel; as one might say politically correctly. I think just because we are in chairs doesn't mean we have to dress down or be second-rate citizens. I just wish we had better representation.

\\

I am so very excited because I am going down to San Diego on Friday. This will be my first solo trip since the stroke. Will the plane flight go ok? Will the accommodations work out ok? So, so many questions. Some would call me a worry wart; some would call me spoiled. The answer to them is that I have my preferences and I just want everything to go in an orderly fashion.

I am going down to visit one of my really good friends and my sorority sister from college, Tiffany. Tiffany is the type of friend that I can tell anything to. She is the type of friend that I can be driving down the road with and have this incredible flight of ideas and I can say, "Do you think that caterpillars really have six legs?" And she will respond like, "You know, I have often thought of that myself and I think so." That's what I mean with Tiffany; we are just on the same wavelength. But two people couldn't have grown up more differently. Where as I was brought up in a middle class background and had parents that were always together, Tiffany didn't have that. But she still pursued her goal, which was to go to law school. She, right now, is in Law school down in San Diego. I am really proud of her. Some think that pride is something that can be only seen in families-but I don't think that's true. I am truthful with her and she back with me. It is really a great relationship. If one of us looks fat in an outfit the other just has to say so, and it is like no big thing.

While I'm down there (San Diego is about a one hour plane ride from Sacramento) I am going to see Jenn Palmer who is also a sorority sister. Although Jenn and I weren't as close, I still feel right at home with her. God, I made some wonderful friends at UC Davis. Anyway, I think Tif and I will see Jenn on Friday night with Aaron and his girlfriend.

Aaron is a friend of my brother's-a college friend. He and his family have been around through thick and thin. My mother and I visited San Diego just after I had been let out from the hospital. Boy-what a difference they have seen in me! The Ritchies, Aaron's family, are really babes and they have an elevator in their house so if anything goes wrong with our hotel we can always stay there-but I don't speculate that anything will go wrong.

I will go with my trusty Mom to the Sacramento airport where she will make sure I get on the plane all right and then it will be in the hands of Tiffany. It's not that I don't trust Tiffany it's just that what if... nobody is there... what if.

The Beginning of the Next Week

Oh my God! I hope Holiday Inn rots and burns in Hell! I feel a lot of animosity towards them at the moment. Let me explain. Please. Ok, I got down to San Diego on Friday. I was a tad anxious because nobody came to meet me on the plane. I thought, oh great! I get down here and I am supposed to have two people waiting for me and nobody shows up. But, I was wrong. I got off the plane with the help of a strong stewardess who, by the way, had a cousin who had a stroke. We were in a deep discussion about it and she was fully ignoring her other passengers, but I didn't even notice that the passengers were all off until it was my turn. And I am always the last person to exit because I use a wheelchair.

Before I get too engrossed with my San Diego tale, let me tell you about this stewardess. Planes are always one of the hardest for me. I don't know what it is but my voice has the volume but not the intonation or something. But whenever I get on a plane, with the engine noise it is really difficult to understand me so I normally just retreat into my headphones. This time was different in that I didn't have my headphones because this was my first solo flight and my Mom didn't want anything to hinder my transfer from the plane seat to the chair. So the stewardesses took pity on me and tried to talk to me. I can always tell that they have no clue as to what I am saying because their shakes and nods of the head constantly come at the wrong time. But with this stewardess, I made an extra effort to speak up and although the whole plane could hear our conversation it was very informative. She said her cousin, Julie, had suffered a stroke that also affected her right side and

89

consequently her voice. The stewardess said that Julie had a boy that was four and she was on her second marriage and she was only twenty-six years old! I said, "So, there is hope!", but I really thought, oh good God!

All in all, it was really good to talk to the stewardess and it was even better to find out that there is more than one person out there who is young and who has had a stroke. I gave the stewardess my email address, but to this day, I have not heard a word from Julie.

So, anyway, where was I? Oh yes, I had just gotten off the plane and I was really anxious but when I got to the top of the platform-there was Tif- coming towards me like a burst of light (Aaron was stuck in traffic and met us at the luggage retrieval). Tif and I hugged and it was like good old times. When Aaron met up with us I kind of felt bad for him-but not too bad.

When we got my bag Aaron rolled it to the car. You see, Aaron's family has a fetish for exotic cars so I got to ride in a brand new Bentley while Tif followed in her new Saturn. She used to have a Colt but, God rest its soul, she had to trade it in. We had fun, fun times in that Colt but now she has another car. But once again, I am getting off of the subject.

I met Tif and then we proceeded down in the elevator which was pretty hard to find and then once we'd found it and used it we had the worst time with people trying to come on when we were just trying to get off. That is one thing about being in a wheelchair, nobody sees you. It seems as though everybody has tunnel vision. They don't look down! You would be surprised!

Like I was saying, Aaron came and we wheeled my bag out to his waiting car. I had forgotten the handicapped placard but it was ok. Instead, that weekend I awed Tif and Aaron with my amazing acrobatic abilities!

They made so much fun of my bag because it was rather large in size. Well, I couldn't help it because when you are traveling normally, you have all sorts of extraneous crap. When you are traveling in a wheelchair multiply that by three. You are afraid that you are going to leave something and gone are the days when you can just would run back to the plane and get the thing you forgot. So, consequently, I packed everything and what a big suitcase I had! In my defense, I had to dress for hot and cold and dressy and not so dressy. It is such a pain being fashionable. And I had three bottles of wine! Can't forget the wine.

First stop was Kensington to visit Aaron's niece who was five months old. She was really precious but the amazing thing was that Aaron just gave the baby to me. I mean, I can hold a baby but all of the mothers are very suspicious and protective. Aaron just gave me the baby without even a second thought. I have held one other baby since the stroke and I think now, watch out!

After we saw the baby (did I mention that she was precious?) we went to the Holiday Inn and we checked into our smoker's room. When I made the reservations, the hotel told me that they only had smoking room's left. They made it seem like they had another non-smoking room. I just assumed that the other disabled room was taken but oh no, there were two disabled rooms and they both happened to be smoking. Can we say discrimination? They assume that since we are disabled that we don't matter! On the contrary, my needs are just as important. In fact, I am very fragile (sarcasm); my needs are even more important.

So, Tiffany and I were a little peeved but we thought that we wouldn't let Holiday Inn ruin our time together. Plus, we had dinner that night with Aaron, Aaron's girlfriend, Jenn, Edward (Aaron's brother), and that is it.

But our room did have that underlying nicotine stench that penetrates your clothes and is impossible to remove you or the room- even with oodles and scads of room refresher (which they used).

So, we thought, oh well-we pre-partied with Jenn instead of worrying about it. That night we went out to a nice, nice restaurant called Il Piccolo. The waiter was speaking in Italian except for when he came to me and then I responded with "Thank you" in Italian but he responded with "Your welcome" in French thinking nobody would understand. But I responded with, "Do you speak French?" in French. I really took him aback. We proceeded to have a rather lengthy conversation in French. He at the last moment gave me his restaurant's email and told me to email him some pictures. I didn't really think anything of it until two mornings later at the Ritchie's house, Dave Ritchie, the father, was telling Tif, Jen, and me that Roberto (the Italian waiter that spoke French) was asking about me in their conversation. I got it in my head that Roberto was the man for me; leave out the fact that I couldn't remember what he looked like. So, I emailed him but I never got an answer. He was probably married or something horrid like that. I am now the "other woman." Yeah right, in my dreams.

Anyway, we had a very pleasant dinner and after that Aaron and Edward and Susie (Aaron's girlfriend) dropped us off at the hotel in a red Ferrari and a silver Rolls-Royce. Nice! Tif and I had to come back to the horrible smoker's room and we found out (because we decided to look at it) that the shower was far from adequate. The shower chair that I was supposed to sit on was permanent and it was placed about 5 feet from the controls. Hello! How am I supposed to take a shower on my own? We were too tired to deal with anything that complicated until we had some sleep. I was just coming down from the adrenalin rush from just taking my first solo trip since the "accident" and Tif was just coming off of law school finals. It was a deadly combo-for sleep, I mean.

The next day Tif and I went to the mecca of all malls-Fashion Valley. I proceeded to shop away all of my money. Oh well! I've REALLY got to stop doing that! But Tiffany and I did see Chocolat. This movie that won all sorts of Academy Awards. It was quite good plus, I even liked it better than the book, which I read.

We got back to the smoker's room around 7:30 p.m. and we decided to see what we could do about the shower chair situation. We called the front desk and they said they were sending maintenance around. When maintenance got there we found that the maintenance guy barely spoke English and he was basically incapable of even changing a light bulb (which had also burned out). We then saw a placard that said, "If you are not satisfied with your stay, inform management and we will try to make your stay better. If we cannot do anything we will refund your money." This was all that Tif and I needed to see. So, Tif marched down to the office where she met the ogre-like manager who said that there was nothing she could do and that they were completely in the ADA requirements. Uh, I don't think so! I know the ADA pretty damn well and I know they were not inside requirements. And the whole thing about it was that she would not refund our money. She WOULD NOT.

Tif and I discussed the problem and decided to call the manager one more time and the manager said if we wanted to leave we could and she would only charge us for one night. Thank you so, very much!

The only problem with the whole situation was that I really need a handicapped bathroom. For showers and for the toilet. So, we were kind of stuck between a rock and a hard spot. We decided to call Aaron and see what he had to say. He informed us that we should get the Hell out of there and that he would be over in an hour to pick us up. That gave me enough time to take a shower. It was a wee bit humbling because I had to sit on the shower chair and there was no way I could even remotely think about using the controls since they was 5 feet away. Tif then had to basically give me the shower head (since it was detachable) and then let me shower. Like I said, it WAS humbling but it was only Tif.

When I got through I was nice and clean and Aaron was there. Tif, Aaron, and I went to check out and I had another lengthy conversation with the manager, this time only over the phone because she was smart enough to get the Hell out of there. Do I say Hell too much? She wouldn't give us our money back so I had to pay for one night, unsatisfied.

Aaron and I hopped in the red Ferrari and zoomed off (but not before I informed the night attendant that he was dealing with two Law students, Tif and Aaron) and making sure to give a little honk so the night attendant could see what kind of car we were in and report back to the manager. At least, that's what we hoped would happen.

Tif followed us in her car but it was about 9:00 by that time and we were really starving. So, we had decided before our departure from the Holiday Inn where we would eat. We decided on this little Mexican place where I drowned my sorrows with margaritas. Big mistake! I could drink a lot before the hemorrhage but now two drinks and I am drunk. I know I am a lightweight, but what can I say? See, the whole problem is that I'm a gulper not a sipper. And that night was definitely NO exception. I had no place to stay and the whole weekend was turning out to be a big flop.

Aaron suggested that we stay with him. Duh! His family had an elevator in their house so it was the only logical place. The only reason we didn't stay there in the first place was because it wasn't wheelchair accessible-granted they had the elevator, but not the shower and bathroom facilities that I need. Plus, we didn't want to intrude upon them. But we ended up intruding upon them anyway. I had no pride left.

By the time we got there it was later than 12:00 and my drunkenness was starting to wear off and tiredness was starting to set in. I asked Aaron very politely where my bed was (I was sharing with Tif so I should say our); it was Aaron's room because the guest room was down a few stairs. Obviously, that was no good because of the wheelchair. We settled into Aaron's room and after I had done my nightly rituals of my various ablutions I fell into bed and was asleep within three minutes.

The next morning, we woke up and I was, amazingly enough, not hung over. I was as fresh as a mountain flower-or so they say in Switzerland. We proceeded up (Tif and I took the elevator) to breakfast where Aaron and his parents were waiting. I had a long reunion with Mr. and Mrs. Ritchie and then we waited for our breakfast which consisted of bagels and scrambled eggs. The maid went out to get the bagels as we looked out over the Western coastline. Their house is situated on the ocean so we looked at the various surfers while we waited. They turned my wheelchair around to face the surf and it was quite nice! Jenn ended up coming over for breakfast and we ate and then said our goodbyes. Then Tif and I went to Seaside. We walked around and ended up eating at this place called Oceanfront View. It was Tif's birthday in a few weeks, so when she went to the restroom I motioned to the waitress. When she came over I ordered a piece of cheesecake to come with candles on it. When it came, the waitress and I sang her Happy Birthday. The only problem was that the candles kept blowing out, so I remedied the problem and told Tif to touch my outstretched finger and make a wish. God, I can really think quickly in an otherwise desperate situation!

After the late lunch, I hopped on my plane and flew back up to Northern California-back to my regular life and back to school.

You know, it was really fun visiting Tiffany and seeing Aaron and Jen, so, I was sorry to come home. There was so much that went on (both good and bad). I was kind of like, "Oh, yes, I get to go home!". I guess you know what works in the specific area that you live in. I know what is going to happen in Davis. I know what is accessible and what isn't, so when you add a new town to the recipe, it is complete chaos. Take San Diego, for instance. They boast that it is the most accessible town in the U.S. I didn't get that impression at all. At every turn, it seemed like there was some sort of barrier. If I lived there, I'm sure that I would know where to go. That is why I don't necessarily like traveling-but in the same regard I am drawn to it with an irresistible force. It is a predicament!

May whatever

I am graduating. Finally. It's taken six long years. I've finally done it. Seriously, I would have given up a long time ago if it weren't for my Mom and my Dad but mostly my Mom. I remember after the first quarter back (taking only one class and with my Mother accompanying me). I wanted to take a break but my Mother gave me an emphatic "No" and that was the end of the story. I often, to myself and to others, thank my Mother for her steadfastness because I would have never stuck through it if it weren't for her. Now I am the biggest intellectual snob there is. I plan to have a big, big party with 80 or 100 people. All of my closest friends! The list started out rather small but I kept saying, "Oh, but I have to invite them." The list, therefore, is quite large. I am inviting a lot of my college buddies and a few from the crowd of people that I have met since the stroke.

I have this one friend named Debra who I have met since the stroke. I had her in my very first class back at UC Davis. I didn't know her that well in History (that was the class that we had together) but I do remember wondering about her in the discussion that we opted to take for one unit. And then I had her again in Political Science and we got to talking and then we made a coffee date at this place called Chocolat. She said she could remember the first thing I said to her. Well, it was really not the first thing but it was one of the first. Let me give you some background. Everybody thinks that I am some timid creature when they first meet me but then I open my mouth and their preconceived ideas are proven false. So, I was asking her how she had done in this one Economics class that had my mother and me looking at each other in utter dumbfoundedment. Is dumbfoundedment a word? Anyway, I was asking her how she had done and she said she had received an A. The first thing out of my mouth was, "you dork face." She then turned to my mom and said, "Did she just call me a dork face?" I guess we knew we were compatible then. But Debra is so like me, our sense of humor and everything. We both enjoy coffee and pastries and people watching; that's why we are so compatible. She spent her junior year abroad in Israel and I spent part of mine in France. We can just be around each other and not say a word because we are content in each other's presence.

Katie is another friend who is like "is this girl for real?" I first met her in a French class. She approached me and asked if I was from Yuba City. She is from Yuba City also, but she has made a metamorphosis from a once shy, timid girl that I remember in high school to a self-assured, radiant young woman that I know in college. In high school, I knew who she was but I didn't know her. I remember her in a hooded sweat-shirt in high school sticking warily to the wall. She went to Belgium for the year in between high school and college where I suspect she bloomed. Whereas before a guy would just pass her by on the street without a second glance, now they would stop and stare. If you were to confront her with these observations she would deny all of them. See, that's the type of person she is. She is so damn caring, thoughtful, and sincere; if I could just have one ounce of her personality. If I could just be like her... the world would be a much brighter place. I am very tainted. But the cold, hard fact remains-I am not like her.

And then there is Nicole. I won't even go into how extremely great Nicole is. I will give one example. We were driving down the road one day. I was singing and I got the lyrics to this song that was on the radio totally bass ackwards. Instead of saying something negative she said, "Oh, don't worry about it. The words were too slow." I thought, whoa. My brothers and sister would have made unparalleled fun of me. That just the kind of chick she is. Caring!

I had my graduation party and it was a blast. I had 80 + people there. About 2/3 of the people were kids I had known from school and who currently go there. The other 1/3 of the people were adults and some of my friends from home. I also had occupational therapists, physical therapists, speech thera-pists, pastors (although I do not have a faith, I have come to really love this one guy), caregivers, and other odd people. The youngin's mainly stayed outside by the keg while the older people preferred the inside setting a little better.

Before the party, I had a little talk with my parents and I told them that under no condition was I going to be in the wheel-chair for the party. I calmly (well, not so calmly but I like to tell myself that) informed my parents that it was MY party and that I was NOT going to be in the wheelchair. They compromised (good for them because there was no compromising; it was a made decision) and they had me sit on a bar stool where I could greet my guests. Everybody came in and greeted me and told me what a great job I'd done and blah, blah, blah. We had a Mexican theme with salsa, beans, rice, guacamole, tortillas, carnitas, and tamales. I wrestled with my mother over the issue of beer; she wanted the cheaper Bud but I wanted the more expensive keg of Heiniken. Reasoning with her was rather difficult but in the end I won. My argument was: these people (mainly the younger people) are beer drinkers and they will know the difference between cheap and expensive beer.

Ok, back to where I was before I got side tracked and that was where everyone was greeting me and telling me what an inspiration I was to them all and that kind of jazz. I mean, it is great being an inspiration and everything but what I wouldn't give to be just like one of them and not in this stupid wheelchair. People are very thoughtful-to a certain extent. Like, take for instance, my party. All of the younger kids were outside and they wanted me to join them so Kirk (one of my very best friends in the whole wide world) took it upon himself to walk me outside. I walk pretty well if I have my brace on and I haven't had anything to drink (and that night I was abstaining). I just walk as slow as molasses in winter. Kirk didn't care though, so he just got busy and walked me out to the patio. It was kind of funny, this big, tall, blonde guy walking me out to the patio with his little girlfriend, Sarah, barking out orders. But what was even funnier was that as Kirk was walking with me my shirt was riding up to my midriff. I finally said, "Kirk, we have to have a talk." And Kirk looked at me all baffled and then Sarah whispered, "Honey, you are exposing her stomach". And Kirk said, "Sorry, sorry!." It doesn't sound as funny as it was.

So, I finally got outside to where all of the younger people were and I shot the shit with all of my buddies. It was nice hearing how they are doing but it made me want to return to the life when your parents paid all of the bills, you could sleep until noon if you wanted to, and the biggest thing on your mind was what you were going to wear to the fraternity party on Friday night- college life. I guess those days are gone though. It just seems to me that I will be in school forever. Oh well!

The party was a really fun time. At the end of it, all of my sorority, they got a group picture. I know it sounds corny but that's what came about. We had a good many girls in the picture and one girl in my sorority from the University of Arizona and one girl from the University of Southern California. It was a good picture.

Last week we went to Maui-as a graduation trip, for my sister and me because my sister also graduated from high school in Sacramento. It was really very, very fun. But I tell you, if I hadn't had my Dad there I wouldn't have been able to do half the stuff that I did. I know America is supposed to be handicapped accessible but it really isn't. I mean accommodations are but there were barriers wherever I went.

At this one resort we were at, it was all handicapped accessible to a certain extent. It was just a matter of finding the accessibility. It was as if we were in a maze! To get down to the pool, first you had to take the elevator down and then you had to go all of the way down to the eating area. And this was no easy feat because it was a full-on trek to get to the other end of the resort where the eating area was located. Not to mention, the eating area was full of diners most of the time. Then, to actually get down to the pool from the eating area you had to take a path that eventually wound around the pool. Then, you were there. It was a mission to do it in a wheelchair, but if you weren't in a wheelchair and you could walk, it was a matter of going down in the elevator and walking about 20 feet and going down some stairs. But I can't do any kind of stair so it was the roundabout way for me.

One thing that I really grooved with was snorkeling. I was a snorkeling fanatic when I was there. I told all my friends when I got back that I had a new sport of choice. But getting down to the water was another issue altogether. Getting down to the beach should have been no problem all except that there was a really steep incline down to the actual beach. To maneuver this, my father had to get in back of me and pull the chair to give it some leverage and my sister had to get in front of the chair in case it broke away.

Once we got down to the beach it was a different story. My dad had asked the concierge for a manual chair because I had the electric wheelchair. Sure, they provided him with one but it was a ghetto one from the 1970s. So, I would transfer from the electric chair to the manual chair and (I rather liked this part) three buff Hawaiian guys would transport me down to the water. There I was, in full-blown snorkeling gear sans wheelchair in the arms of these Hawaiian males. Like I said, I didn't mind THAT part. What was embarrassing was the whole fact that I had to be carried down to the water. But in these situations, I have learned to swallow my pride. And what made it ten times more embarrassing was that through this whole ordeal I had on my fins, snorkel, mask, and my life jacket.

On Thursday of that week, we went snorkeling off a boat on Molokai. The crew couldn't have been more accommodating but still it was hard. First of all, we, checked in and then we waited until everyone was on the boat and then we got on. We ended up getting on with the wheelchair. What that entailed was a guy up in front of the wheelchair to keep it from doing God knows what and then a guy behind for, I guess, moral support. And then my dad was, of course, pushing me in the borrowed wheelchair. On the way, it was really fun. It was about a two hour journey to Molokai and during the trip everybody was applying sun screen and listening to some hip music.

When we got there everybody (there was about 40 people on the boat) gathered around the captain and listened to him tell us not to touch the sea turtles. Everyone agreed and got in the water and started swimming around. I had called earlier to make sure that they had masks with prescriptions in them. Ever since the hemorrhage I have had to wear glasses and at the thought of not being able to see anything, well, it just made me want to cry. I really wanted to see sea turtles because I had never seen them before.

My dad's anxiety level was at about 100+. Can we say uptight? He is not normally a high-stress kind of guy but on this occasion he was unbearable. I guess I can see where he was coming from. He was worried that I would get caught in coral and above all he was worried about the boat and me being on it and it not being wheelchair friendly. His anxiety was well-founded because once I'd get in the water and start swimming around my mask would fill up with water. This happened for about half hour and then my father said we were going back to the boat to see about another mask. We got there and got another mask but it did the same thing. We went back to the boat a third time and the captain told us that we didn't have the mask down low enough. Well, duh! I could have snorkeled a good deal more if it weren't for this little problem. My Dad and I went out once more and we managed to see 15 sea turtles. One swam close to two feet from my face but we promised that we wouldn't touch it; I was a good girl and didn't.

The sea turtles weren't all big like you'd expect. Most of them that I saw were small. They were nearly one foot in diameter except for the one that swam very close to me; that one was circa five feet in diameter. It was an extraordinary experience.

On the way back, everybody was getting warm because it was very cold in the water. They had a big spread for lunch and everybody dug in. I had a tuna sandwich with red onions and it was so good. I dream about sandwiches like that now. Just for some reason, it was so good; probably the combination of the cold water, the warm sun, and all of the pent-up anxiety.

When we got back to the hotel we literally fell into bed because we had to be ready at 7:00 and that meant we had to be up at 6:00, so we were pretty darn tired. When we woke up we went down to the pool. Then, we had to be ready by 6:30 P.M.

because we were going to some fancy smancy dinner, so we had to shower and put on makeup and the whole deal. Oh, what girls have to go through!

When we got to the restaurant there was no ramp going down to the porch where, of course, my Dad wanted to eat. There were three steps but there was no ramp, so the men at the restaurant rigged up this wooden board to act as a ramp. It was all quite embarrassing. I mean, what you have to do to eat!

The next day we went to Mount Halikali. It is something like the second highest mountain in the U.S.A. I don't really know because, frankly, I wasn't paying attention to that particular lecture from my parents. But we drove and drove and drove. For Christ's sake, I thought Maui was an island-doesn't that mean it is a piece of land floating in water? So, we drove and drove and drove until we finally got there at about 11:00 in the morning. People will advise you to get there at sunrise but two mornings in a row was kind of pushing it. When we finally got up there it was above the cloud cover and it WAS awesome. The only thing was that I HAD to go to the bathroom. Badly. Normally, I take precautions against this kind of thing and go to the bathroom each time before I get in the car to go someplace. But this time was different because we were in the car for so long and there wasn't a place where I could ask my Dad to pull over and I could go to the bathroom. When we got out of the car we went up to this little tourist's station and looked at all of the posters of the lava flows, etc. My Mom got all excited and was saying, "Look, girls. I didn't know that the tertiary soil only cooled down 40 years ago."

My sister was nodding her head and looking at my Mom with rapt attention and then turned to me and said, "Did you see a Starbucks anywhere on the way?".

We then went back to the hotel but before we did we ate lunch at this Chop Suy place. I politely declined. I am what you would call a very adventurous eater but I don't like to eat anything that has a picture corresponding with a number. My Dad was in heaven; you have to understand my Father and that can be a very difficult thing. He loves a good food deal more than anything. Don't get me wrong-he is not cheap at all. He just enjoys a good deal every now and then. The difficult thing about this dive was that the chairs had no back so with my balance (which is compromised to say the least) it was very hard. My Mom ate with her arm through mine and my Dad ate with his arm through my other one. Again, it was quite embarrassing but then again what can a girl do? I should write a book called "Embarrassing Moments of Jane."

Do you know what I find ultra embarrassing? It is when my Mom tries to feed me in public and tries to tuck my napkin in my collar. It is dying material when she does that. This was one occasion that she tried to do that. It is like, " Uh, I am 23 years old and enrolled in a graduate program.". But do you think that means diddly squat to her? Hell no! Once her baby, always her baby.

I sometimes think that having this stroke was good for my Mom and Dad. I know that's rather sadistic to say, and I mean this in the most respectful manner possible. If you think about it, it makes sense. It is just about the time when all of the little "fledglings" are leaving the "nest." One by one, all four of us take the steps to leave home. Me, by going to France, Chuck, by going to law school, Peder and Karin, by eventually going to college, and then this strikes. It is a new activity for my parents to turn their attention to. Seriously. They do treat me like I'm a baby. About 14 months old to be exact. My Dad still cuts my meat and my Mom, like I said, is forever trying to stuff the napkin in my collar. Excuse me. I am a grown, liberated young woman (last time I checked). Apparently not!

It's like this weekend. I had my friend Sarah Wilson (who is one of my best friends and who is an absolute riot) meet me at the Handlery-this hotel in San Francisco on Union Square-for another one of my good friends, Ann's, going away party. My parents decided to beat the traffic and just stay in San Francisco that night and go out to dinner. They were slated to stay in the Carlton, which was about a block from the Handlery. At the last minute, my Dad said, "Check and see if they have a room for us near Janie's room." I said to myself, "No bloody way." We wanted to do some stuff that we didn't want the rents around for. Luckily, there wasn't a room. Too bad!

Instead, before we left for the party, my Mom, Dad, Sarah, and I had a drink at a little Irish Pub on the corner. It was very nice, and before we left my Dad was able to get us in a taxi and tell the driver to take us where we needed to go. Ok, I am getting ahead of myself once again. I was on Hawaii.

You must think I'm horribly spoiled talking about San Diego, Hawaii and San Francisco. But in all actuality, I'm not. I just inherited my Dad's traveling bug. It's a bad thing to have inherited but the up-side of it is that if my Dad has this inkling to go someplace fun and exotic; he has nobody to go with except my mom, my sister, and me. That, my friends, is the up-side of the whole situation. Or, rather, the beauty of the situation.

So, the next day in Hawaii was spent doing essentially nothing. I maneuvered around breakfast which was a buffet (I hate buffets but I made an exception for this one) and then after that out to the pool. Breakfast was another scenario altogether. Breakfast and I had a love/hate relationship. It was this gorgeous ordeal with cheese Danishes, muffins, sweet rolls, granola, yogurt, sausage, omelets, fruit, and the list goes on. After, my sister and I surveyed the spread, we would order our cappuccinos and would embark upon breakfast. I had a little weakness for cheese Danishes, (I would get one of those every morning.) But like I said, the problem with the whole set-up was that it was a buffet. I cannot partake in the true breakfast buffet ceremony with just one good hand. I cannot take whatever I would like and still hold the plate unless I balance the plate on my lap. That is quite precarious because my bad right hand will sometimes want to get a tad crazy on me and try to move in toward my body and whatever is on my plate gets pushed off . So, in this beautiful display of food I had to rely on either my Mother, my Father or my sister. Not that I'm saying there is anything wrong with that! It's just that sometimes I wanted to get a little wild and crazy or just be a wee bit spontaneous (like getting that extra egg). I found that it was difficult to be this way with someone else standing right there. I guess it all boils down to independence. I am a very independent person, therefore I don't care for buffets. But I managed; after the cappuccinos I could face the world.

There was something very, extraordinarily exciting. Hulk Hogan was staying at the same place as us. We saw him every day after water aerobics (which my Dad helped do by steadying me from the back and therefore enabling me to participate in the event. Good old Dad, always there when you need him!). We would then spend the rest of the morning watching him. Intensely productive, don't you think?

This one day a worker (she turned out to be a masseuse) came up to my sister and me and she asked us if we would like a massage. My sister and I looked at each other and said, "Uh, yes!". I think she felt sorry for me because I was in a wheel-chair. I WILL take that kind of sympathy! And the best part about the whole thing was that it was free. If it weren't, then my sister and I would have to pass on it. We would have to do this because we had been feeling liberated and decided to order whatever we liked on room service-and that was beginning to add up. But it was free, so after a quick shower, we came back and met the lady in our designated spot. Instead of paying, we bought our masseuse an ice cream bar (on room service, of course). We found out that her name was Linda and she had a friend in Berkeley (about one hour from Davis) who did acupuncture. I am not one for sticking needles all over in my body but I consulted with my Mom (whose mantra is, "What the hell, it can't put us back anymore than we already are.") And she was great guns so I thought I had better call him. I still haven't, but I plan to-I just haven't gotten the courage up yet.

But anyway, she massaged my feet and legs until they were putty and it felt good! To send her on her way with a smile on her face, I ordered her a Mango Margarita (on room service again, of course). I looked like the great beneficiary but I swear, it's so much easier to spend other people's money. When I ordered her the margarita, my sister just rolled her eyes but I didn't see her complaining as she took a sip of her own!

The rest of the trip went great all except for when we got back into SFO and then shit hit the fan-excuse the crude expression. Before I get into all of that I want to tell you about something else. So, we were coming back on the airplane (obviously) and I had already finished sides three and four on my cassette player, so I decided to watch Mystic Pizza which was playing not on the backside of the chair in front of us but on the television up on the roof of the plane. I happened to have a seat about five rows from the television set and, I swear, I couldn't see the damn thing. It looked like faceless bodies moving around the screen. It was so irritating. I just had to look at the Sky Mall catalog the two hours I had remaining on the bloody plane. I never wore glasses before the hemorrhage but, obviously, I do have to wear them now. This particular prescription was old and I was having it replaced with a new one once I got home. That was a long time without anything to do. I got thoroughly bored.

So, as you might have imagined I was ready when San Francisco came into view. I was ready to get off that plane and go to bed. I knew we had about another two hours or so by the time we had gotten our luggage and met the airporter. Like the good girl that I am. I let all of the other people off of the plane first, all the while imagining my comfy bed. We (my Dad and I) finally managed to get through the amazingly narrow seats (we were in row 21 and the exit was in row 7) we then had to stand there and stand there to wait for the wheelchair. Not an uncommon thing to have to do but tiresome for an already tired girl, and they were taking an awfully long time. Then, a steward asked one guy from cargo where my wheelchair was because we had been waiting for about a half hour. The cargo guy muttered something and walked away quickly with his head down. My Mom was saying how this couldn't be good when we saw the people in black coats walk up to us. I swear, it looked like something out of the Godfather or something. It looked as if we had taken our last breaths because we were going to get shot. My Mom later told me that she was sure that my brothers (whom we had left at home because they "needed to work for a living" (I don't know why my sister and I had to go. Could it be that we get along with my Dad?) had been hideously killed. She was imagining a horrid car wreck or something of the sort but-oh no-worse. It turns out that the black coats came to tell us that my chair had been dropped off the conveyor belt and was now lying motionless on its side without a wheel. When I heard the news, I let out a primordial scream that I didn't know I even possessed.

You may think that a wheelchair being broken is no big thing but to me it's a huge thing. As much as I absolutely hate to admit it, it is a part of me. Wherever I go, my wheelchair is right there with me. I knew this couldn't be good-I knew that I would probably have to use the manual wheelchair for about a month or so; and I hate the manual wheelchair. I was NOT a happy camper. I don't like the manual chair because it is light-about 30 pounds as opposed to the electric chair that is about 250 pounds and isn't electric. Electricity is my access to the outside world. I know I sound like a prisoner but it is kind of like that.

After my primordial scream, the lady in the black coat was doing everything in her power to calm me down, so she offered us each $400 in free, transferable airline vouchers. Between my sniffles I graciously accepted.

When we finally got to the airporter it was about one o'clock and I wasn't in the mood for anything out of the ordinary plus I was being pushed around the airport in an airport wheelchair whose sides didn't even come up by a guy named David who could barely speak English. On top of it all, there were no Starbucks open that late-and that put me in an extra foul mood. Anyway, like I was saying, when we finally got back to the airporter we discovered that he hadn't even brought the correct vehicle to get an electric chair in. So, what

I am trying to say is that if the electric chair hadn't been damaged we would have been staying at the airport hotel until another van with wheelchair access could be sent.

On the ride home, I had a peculiar way of sitting/lying that gave some respite to my bottom, which was majorly starting to hurt. I was sitting so that my seat belt was still fastened but I was lying down to the left. From my waist up I had my head propped on my wheelchair cushions-not optimum but whatever works! That was how I rode back from the San Francisco Airport (about one and a half hours) but I felt bad for my parents who had to go back to Yuba City and work the next day. My Dad is kind of psycho if you were wondering.

The next day, I awoke without my wheelchair (of course) and I found out through my Dad that my wheelchair was being considered "fatally wounded" and they were going to buy me a new one. I thought, whoa, because electric wheelchairs aren't cheap. They set you back a car price or so. You can imagine my surprise. I guess my Dad asked the wheelchair repairman if he would let his daughter go on the streets with a wheelchair that was repaired and once had suffered the damages that mine had. When my Father got the negative answer that was all that he needed to hear. Needless to say, I was going to get a new wheelchair.

I was slated to get the measurements for my new chair just after the 4th of July (nothing moves quickly in the wheelchair business). Just the measurements, mind you. I had been without my chair for two weeks and I estimated that I would be without it for three-four more weeks. I was without it until the first week in September. Like I said, nothing moves fast in the wheelchair business

For the 4th of July, I went home to Yuba City. It's not like I don't have fond memories of Yuba City. Because I do. It's just that there is nothing there for me. I feel like a traitor saying this, but it's the truth. In Davis, I am free to go out. The campus and downtown are just ten minutes away by wheelchair. Compare that to Yuba City where we live 15 miles south of town and where I can't even get down the driveway. It is a no brainer. I bet you are wondering what I mean by I can't get down the driveway. You see, our house is set back a ways and my parents refuse to pave the driveway. Why you ask? Because my parent's reasoning is that they can hear us coming down the driveway. If it is late at night they have the cue to look at their clock and catch us in the process of breaking our curfew-that is, if it was passed. We also live on ten acres mainly consisting of walnut trees and the land between them for the most part is disked. And you had just try to get through disked-up land in a wheelchair. It is a no-can- do.

Yuba City is a very rural community. You get a good number of people who haven't attended college; in Davis (a university town), you get a good deal of overflow from the university working around town. In Yuba City, I get a lot of "Huhs" from store clerks and then the various store clerks ask the person who I'm with what I am trying to say. I remember this one time I was in a yogurt shop in Yuba City and the waitress was having a hard time understanding me. So instead of asking me to repeat myself she says to the girl I'm with, "What is she trying to say?". I let her have a tongue-whipping. If you ever come across a person with a voice disability, DO NOT ASK THE PERSON WHO THEY'RE WITH WHAT THEY ARE TRYING TO SAY. In Davis, there have been few times when the person didn't under-stand me but they calmly asked me to repeat myself. What I am trying to say, is that I am a live person and I demand respect! Way to assert yourself, Jane.

Anyway, like I was saying before I got side-tracked, I went home for the 4th of July. We had a nice barbecue with some family friends (who are babes) and lit off fireworks. In Yuba City, you can still purchase fireworks. Hence, you can burn your house down with relatively no cash!

It was basically uneventful. We went out on the boat to Lake Orville and the big news about town was that the temper-ature had reached over 100 degrees so the local jeweler was going to give back all of the money that he collected from June

15th onward (a promotion). That is how small Yuba City is.
People actually get excited about this kind of crap! Ok, ok-I
admit I was a tad bit excited. After the 4th of July, I just came
back to Davis and did my thing-which didn't consist of much.
I was supposed to get a rental chair from this company. After a
couple of grueling sessions on the phone with these people, I
finally got through to them that I wanted to actually spend some
money with their company. The wheelchair was supposed to be
delivered on the 6th of July to Davis. I got the wheelchair (after
they had tried to deliver it to Yuba City) and I put a big grin on
my face because I thought (the key word being thought) that I
was back in business. I said good-bye to the wheelchair rental
guy and went back to doing my hair with Virginia (a lady who
is a babe and comes for four hours in the morning to do my hair
and walk with me). When we finally got around to transferring
into the chair and starting it up we found that there was
something terribly wrong with it. It had stripped gears and
when I would go, for instance, two feet it would stop dead in its
tracks and make this funky grinding sound and then lurch
forward again. It was all very distressing. I thought, why can't
they just give me a decent chair?

   I got directly on the phone again with this certain company
and told them they had a big problem with their chair and I
needed it fixed right away. It was all, "Oh, I'm sorry, ma'am,"
and, "It won't happen again, ma'am." I thought, finally,
someone knows what I'm going through and will try to fix the
problem. Boy, was I wrong. Even though I had specifically
asked again, that the repairman come to Davis, they sent the
repairman to Yuba City-again. Now, you want to talk about
brain dead, really below average? My sociology class didn't
even compare to the idiots I was dealing with here. When I
finally got it through their thick skulls that my house was
actually in Davis and got them to come over and take a look at
it, they declared that it had gone haywire and they had better
replace the chair with something new. Ooh, the knowledge it
took to make that supposition was immense. They made it

110

known to me that the wheelchair needed to go in for some repairs and that, "Oh no, don't worry, we will send you another wheelchair that is even better but it is a little smaller."

When I got the next chair, I noticed it was a little smaller. But upon further inspection, I noticed it was really small. They had given me a child's chair! Can you believe that? A child's chair! I was so disgusted that I didn't do anything. I barely fit in the chair, it was tight but I thought, oh Hell, because I wasn't about to go another week without an electric wheelchair. I "sucked it up."

Next, we went to Clearlake. If you know anything about California you will know that Clearlake is the second largest lake in California and its beauty is surpassed by none (sarcasm). We have been going to Clearlake since I was born and my mother has been going since she was seven years old. Why they picked Clearlake for a destination I will never fully know but it is a whole lot of fun. I can honestly say that. You see, Clearlake is a 180 degree opposite vacation than Maui. You don't take a shower for the whole week and when you start to smell an odor emanating from yourself you just jump in the late. It is great fun.

This year, we rented a new place in Lakeport and I was all excited for the week. Then we pulled into the house and it was great, all except that it was two stories. Now, how un-wheelchair accessible can you get? My Mom got all wide-eyed and sai "I told you." Funny, Mom, I don't seem to remember you mentioning that. But I let it pass because it wasn't just our family, it was both my aunts and all three of my uncles and all of their families. But for the whole week I had to walk up and down the stairs with a handrail but I had to have somebody there for stability and to make sure that there was a chair at the other end. What was good was that my Dad had the foresight to bring a wheelchair of my grandma's (God rest her soul) and then we had one wheelchair for upstairs and one for downstairs.

But the real hummdinger was that I couldn't even get in the bathroom with my wheelchair (either one). We saw a problem and faced it head on. We decided that my walking into the bathroom each time would never work, so we just took the door off! We, instead, rigged up a sheet. It didn't do the whole job but it was good enough. It was kind of funny going by the bathroom and seeing a sheet there instead of a door.

Even though we took the door off, it was still a tight fit. The whole week I felt as though I would bother somebody if I had to go to the bathroom. I certainly couldn't go by myself because, for one thing there were no bars and for another, the bathroom was set up in a way so that as you went in, the toilet was on the far left facing a wall and against the far wall there was a bathtub. Each time I went to the bathroom I thought I was going to fall into the abyss known as the bathtub. I like baths but not that much! It was kind of funny being there when my Mom was trying to corral me because my mom is only 5 feet 5 inches and I am 5 feet 11 inches (my mom calls me the too big baby). What was my Mom going to do if I really started to fall? Get hurt.

Another thing about this house was that it had what we fondly began to refer to as the "Delores Claiborne Stairs." It had these stairs that disappeared into nothing. Well, I shouldn't really say nothing, because they did lead down into another room that nobody wanted to sleep in or even be in. It had no windows and it had a faint musky smell that reminded us of a bomb shelter. So, we nicknamed it "The Bomb Shelter." Now, we had "The Delores Claiborne Stairs" and "The Bomb Shelter." Anyway, these stairs were at the end of this hallway and I was so deathly afraid that I was going to be going and head right down the stairs.

Apart from all of the swimming, reading, sleeping, we basically did nothing. One day, I think it was Tuesday, only my Aunt Beanie (I will explain the name later), my Mom, my sister, and I were there so, we decided to go for a drive. We hopped in my aunt's new Passat that she was so proud of and we went to Kelseyville to try and do some wine tasting. What were we thinking? This was Clearlake and there isn't much at

Clearlake. So, as you might have imagined, we didn't do any wine tasting. Instead, we just tasted. Period. After we drove around for a while, we settled on some rinky-dink pizza parlor that my mom and my aunt remembered from girlhood. My sister and I went along with it; we thought we had better indulge them a little.

Aside from truly terrible pizza, the bathroom was not too bad. All except for a drop that left you wondering if there was going to be a toilet down there to rest your tush on. You see, handicapped bathrooms must have the toilet a certain height higher than the average bathroom. I am rather spoiled because both my home in Yuba City and my house in Davis have higher toilets. When my Mother and Father were deciding what to do with our home, etc., they nuked the bathroom. There used to be a bathtub in Yuba City but there is now a nice roll-in shower in its place. That's what you get for having decisive parents. When we bought the house in Davis, it was amazingly accessible until you got to the master bath. That was horrors. So, they nuked it too. Just like that. I think I like the bathroom in Davis more because the shower is more compact. Less room to fall and hit your head.

Like I was saying, this bathroom in the pizza parlor was amazingly accessible and I thought to myself, this could be a good experience, but when I went out of the bathroom my eye caught something that it missed on the way in. Lining the walls were pictures of the graduating classes from Kelseyville High. They looked like a bunch of hoodlums. And the girls were scantily clothed, to say the least. My sister and I just stopped and stared. Finally, my Mom had to say something to get us going. We may be from Yuba City but my sister and I are horrible snobs.

Oh, and by the way, we took the rest of the pizza home to eat the next day but we used it for duck food! Don't ever accuse us of being wasteful.

That night my Dad was slated to arrive so I was very anxious. My Dad and I have a special bond that started on the day I arrived (which happened to be on his birthday). I think I've mentioned this. He was also going to bring my grandma's old wheelchair for the downstairs portion of the house. My Dad is also more sympatico (see, a big word, and not even in English) than my Mom when it comes to walking. Since I am not allowed to walk on my own, I have to rely on the good graces of my mom, dad, and sister. My sister leaves for college next month, and it's not like my mom is lazy or anything, she just worries about me taking a tumble with her and she not being able to do anything. My mom is always going, "What if you break your arm or something?". My theory is that you won't get anywhere if you don't try. I am constantly rolling my eyes at what my mom is waggling her finger at me for. Maybe I shouldn't roll my eyes as much and listen to her warning. Maybe not.

My dad didn't end up coming until very late that night and to make up for his delay he was going to go with us for a boat ride the next day. My dad bought us a boat and everything but he doesn't like to ride in it. Go figure. So, his presence greatly honored us. But to get out to the boat was a feat in itself, that is, for me. I had to first get out of my chair because the dock had four or five stairs leading up to it. When I got up there, I wanted to walk a little because I was in my chair an awful lot that week. So, I had to grab onto the railing with my left hand and have my dad hold my right arm (my mom wasn't strong enough to do this) and then I could walk until we got to the part leading down. The only problem with this walking was that the railing was a wee bit short. I would be walking along and I would look over to my left and see rocks, seaweed, water, and fish. It was a little bit disconcerting. When we got to the part that led down, my mom had to tie a ski rope onto the front part of the wheelchair which my sister had shimmied up to the dock. Anyway, we had to tie a water ski line to my chair. That was ultra embarrassing. But apart from being embarrassing I had to be really trusting. Fortunately for me, it was my dad, but all I could do was make funny remarks. You see, my dad had to balance the wheelchair on the back two wheels and pull me down backwards while my mom applied resistance at the top.

When we got back, it was the same routine but in reverse. When I got back into the house, I didn't have the gumption to make it upstairs to my little room so, my dad (the babe) kind of took my room downstairs to me. I already said that we had a bomb shelter kind of room on the downstairs portion of the house, so all my dad did was bring my tape recorder (I get any unabridged book I want on tape through the Library of Congress) and something for me to change into because I was still in my swimsuit. I listened to tapes for less than an hour and then I fell asleep for three hours. The nap was truly delicious! I felt so revitalized!

That is one thing about my brain hemorrhage. It zapped my energy. Whereas before I used to be an eight hour a night kind of girl, now I am a ten hour a night kind of girl. Before, I could go skiing, hiking, and ice skating all in one day, now, I can go three wheel biking and that will take me a week to recover from. It is a bad situation. The whole thing is a bad situation. But it is what I have been offered-this is not a pick and choose kind of deal. Now that I have that off my chest we can go back to the story.

The next day my dad had to go home but he would be back on Friday with my little brother. On Friday, we (my aunt, my mom, my sisters, and) went to lunch at this little Mexican place on the water that was surprisingly good. I was in a MOOD because my mom and sister didn't want to walk me in with the Weanie Walker, It is really called the Winnie Walker but one day my dad wasn't paying attention to what he was saying and he said, "Go and get the thing-you know the Weanie Walker." And from that day on it became known as the Weanie Walker. You know, one of those pet names. The Weanie Walker is this contraption that is a walker but it has a hydraulic braking system and it has opened up the world to me. I walk every-where, though granted, I am slow. So very slow. I don't think you understand. When you think slow, take that, and multiply it by two, and that is how slow I am. I am really slow.

But anyway, there I go getting off on a tangent again. So, I was saying that I was in a MOOD because I couldn't walk in with the Weanie Walker because my mom and my sister were not in the mood. Normally, I would have made them get in the mood but I said to myself, they are on vacation. So instead, I was just in a MOOD. Am I saying mood too much? But I got out of it quickly when the food arrived because it was so good. My aunt and I had the carnitas soft tacos and they were mmm, mmm good.

We came back to the house and my mom and sister took a power nap. I foolishly didn't because I was in a good part of my book on tape. A really good part. And that couldn't wait for a nap. God forbid. So, I didn't take a nap when I should have. All of my cousins and my brother and one of my brother's friends were supposed to come over that night. We waited until about 10:00 at night and just about the time that I was going to bed they arrived. They got hung up in Napa because my cousin, Kate, got a speeding ticket in her new car. The second one in 18 months. She, needless to say, didn't tell her dad that night. I wonder if she ever did tell him.

When I finally went to bed at 11:00 my cousin Chickie (another bizarre name that I will explain later) who is 16 was leading a Congo line around the living room and down the hall. Again, needless to say, they (the whole group of them) were aided in this fortuitous undertaking by a whole slew of beers. They came by my room and I thought to myself, please don't let them come in my room. This was about 1:00 in the morning. They did not end up coming in my room for some odd reason, but I don't ask, "Why?" I noticed the next day there were a lot of dark sunglasses being worn and nobody was quite Johnny-on-the-spot.

That was the day that we had to move out and people weren't moving too fast. But we did end up getting out of there an hour early. On the ride home my mom, dad, and I rode in the same car and it was kind of tense because we couldn't find the electrical hook up for the boat. I, instead, was instructing my dad how to do hand signals for stop, right, and left. That went over like a lead balloon but Hey, I tried.

When we got home I took an ultra power nap and right when I was getting up my best girlfriend from home, Susi, called. She now lives in San Francisco and she was up for the weekend with her new beau who I still hadn't given the stamp of approval. She said she would be over in a half hour. Normally, pre-avm, it would have been enough time. But after the hemorrhage, everything is much more slow. I got off the phone and screamed for my mom. I hadn't taken a shower in a week and I had only washed my hair once. I was truly a sight. If I could have washed myself in a half hour I sure would have but a good shower with a blow dry takes me a good 2 hours. We were dealing with limited time so, I had my mom just wash my hair and I stayed clothed. As it was, I didn't have time to put on any makeup. She came, right on time, and we talked because I was actually going to San Francisco the next weekend for my good friend's going away party. I gave her boyfriend the stamp of approval and she left.

The next weekend arrived and I had a hotel room booked at the Handlery in San Francisco. I was supposed to meet my good friend Sarah Wilson there. The night before my dad had an anxiety reaction and asked me if I could book a room for him and my mom at the same hotel. There was no way in Hell that I was going to book a room at the same hotel, so I booked one at a hotel around the corner. When we got to Union Square there was, of course, nowhere to park so, my dad stayed in the car while my mom got me checked in. While my dad was IN the car, a cop tried giving him a ticket for illegally parking. The ONLY reason we were parked there in the first place was that there was nowhere to get me out. We had to go up the sidewalk as it was to find a curb cut. And if you know San Francisco the least little bit, you will know that is no easy feat. There were cars swooshing past us. I felt bad because my mother had to push me (remember the electric chair was broken) and take her own life in her hands, as well as mine. But, really, what are you going to do?

When we got checked into the room my mom said good-bye and she and my dad went to check into their OWN room at their OWN hotel. That's when I started to hyperventilate. I was lying on the bed and I thought, what happens if a fire starts? I guess I would tumble off of the bed and try to knock myself out and therefore not able to feel my body being burned to a crisp. What I am trying to say is that this place was nice but it was a firetrap in the worst possible way. So, I laid there for a while and then I thought, no sense in calculating doom. I called people instead. I tried Sarah because I figured she was on the road between her hometown and there was no answer on her cell phone so I called Susi next. I got Susi and told her I would meet her at the Comet Club where Ann, my good friend, was having her surprise going away party.

Do you want know how much my calls were? Well, I am going to tell you anyway, $16! Can you believe that?! But that is another story. I now have a cell phone, which is for the express use of situations like this. Ya right!

My parents ended up calling me first and proposing a little drinky-poo before Sarah got there. You have to realize that Sarah is the worst lagger. She says she will be there at about 6:00 (like she did that night) but you know she will really get there around 8:30 (like she did that night).

My parents and I ended up going to this little Irish pub right next door. It was quite good. I had a glass of white wine-my drink of choice besides a gin and tonic or a vodka and lemonade (it depends on the mood I'm in at the time). Sarah finally got there and we toasted drinks with my parents and then my dad put Sarah and I in a taxi and we were off to the Comet Club. My dad did give the taxi driver a crisp $20 bill and told him to take care of us. That did help but the taxi driver, who didn't speak a word of English, was driving at an extremely high rate of speed. So high that it left Sarah and I scrambling for our seatbelts. When he let us out at Comet Club I felt an instant sense of relief flood over me because we were finally out of the dreaded taxi and we were still alive!

When we got into the Comet Club it was excessively dark. It was so dark I couldn't even see the hand in front of my face. I saw Ann and she was appropriately surprised to see me. But back to it being so dark, it was so dark that I saw this older girl in my sorority and she had her hair up and she was smiling at me. I immediately thought, who is she? Is she a lesbian? I thought because she had short hair (her hair wasn't actually short she just had it up in a clip) she was automatically a lesbian! Boy, did I feel stupid when I found out who she actually was. I recounted the story to Sarah over a late dinner of sushi and she couldn't stop laughing. I felt stupid once again.

After dinner, around 12:00, we went back to the Handlery. But before coming back to the hotel we had to endure another cab ride. This time it was another guy who (surprise!) didn't speak English but he was very nice in the way that he pulled up to a driveway to get me in and he helped in getting me in. He was a very cool guy even if the only way we had to communicate was with various hand gestures.

When we had reached our hotel Sarah and our nice taxi driver were in the process of helping me out when we heard a, "Oh, step away I was in Stanford as a kid, I know what to do". I looked up to see some woman that I had never even met helping me out of a taxi. I was a little bit drunk as was Sarah but I thought, oh no, she is just being nice. I did happen to notice that she was wearing kind of grubby clothes but I chalked that up to it just being dark and me not being able to see and being a tiny bit drunk.

Oh no, nothing like that! As Sarah and I made our way to another Irish pub we saw that she was a transient who proceeded to knock us up for money. I'm sorry, but there is no money here! Sarah and I decided after this and before we made it into the pub that we just wanted to go back to the death trap aka the room.

Earlier in the day we decided to meet my parents the next morning at 10:00 at the Starbucks across the street. We woke up at 9:45 and we scrambled around and we made it down to the Starbucks at 10:10. My parents still weren't there. Wouldn't you know! We hustled back to the room to do some extraneous stuff like-brush our teeth. We were just heading out and before we left Sarah glanced at the book of information and she saw that check out was at 10:00. We had a big problem because we weren't even packed up and ready to go. Once again, I am very slow. How many times do I have to repeat myself!

We had figured that we would pack up after we got back from Starbucks. Whoops! I had Sarah call and give them the big sob story about how I was handicapped and blah, blah, blah and you know what-it worked! It does every time. I don't mean to sound smug and like I am working the "system". Because, I am really not, it's just that being disabled really comes in handy at times like this.

We met my parents at Starbucks. They had gone to another one 2 streets down. I mean, there is a Starbucks, now, on every block. We had a nice breakfast and when we were going to leave I had that overpowering sense of dread knowing that I had to go back to the room and pack up and leave. This vacation was sure short! My parents ended up coming back with Sarah and me to the death trap and helping me pack. It wasn't bad; between the 3 of us it only took about 15 minutes. With just me doing it, it would have taken me an hour at least.

I said my good-byes to Sarah knowing full well that I wouldn't see her for at least 3 months. You have to know Sarah, she is what I affectionately call a frazzler. She is the type that is always pressed for time, always in a rush, and flat-out doesn't have the time to sit down and make a simple phone call.

Well anyway, here comes the good part of my mini-vacation. We were cruising along some street in the middle up San Francisco heading to the Bay Bridge and my dad decides to fix his seatbelt which was all kattywompus. He was in the far left lane on a one way street so that to his left were parked cars-

or so he thought.

He gets the brainy idea to fix his seatbelt by opening up the car door. The traffic was stopped and as he opened up the door a motorcyclist zoomed by on his left and collided with the part of the door that closes onto the inner part of the car. I was just like, "Oh, good God!". I knew better than to open my mouth at a time like this. And as my dad got out of the car and battled with the guy, my mom and I sat huddled in the car being very quiet. When my dad got back in the car, we found out that the guy riding the motorcycle was not hurt and named Xiong; my dad said that he would probably sue us for all we were worth. Again, I kept my mouth shut. We drove home in silence interrupted occasionally by loud outbursts from my dad about San Francisco, traffic, or those damn immigrants.   When I got back to Davis it was work as usual. When I say work it means walking. One time, I was out to dinner and my parents asked me if I wanted a second glass of wine and I had to tell them no because I was walking. My mom said instead of saying I have to drive, I will say I have to walk. This is fitting because I no longer have my license to drive. When I walk it takes a good amount of concentration and when there is any type of alcohol on board it just isn't cute.

In the Spring and Summer I make it a habit to walk outside. I tend to walk more quickly and I get a great tan. Well, I was walking one day and this really cute boy came by and looked back and said "Hello!" I almost fell over. I looked to my left and my right trying to find somebody else but there was nobody. I asked my caregiver, Virginia, if he was talking to me and she affirmed my suspicion. From that point on the mystery boy/man was a big joke between Virginia and I. It wasn't until 3 weeks later that I saw him again and his time he stopped and talked to me.

He told me he was sung and was musically inclined. I, of course, suddenly knew a lot about music when in reality I know squat about music. He was a Music major at UC Davis but he had graduated 3 years ago. When he finally walked away,

Virginia and I were all giggles. That is basically the end to my story. My claim to fame. I know you all wanted me to fall madly in luv with him but nothing ever came of it. I guess it's just fun to have somebody of the opposite sex to imagine about. It isn't nearly as fun when you get to know him.

//

We left for San Diego on a Tuesday and we were staying in this little cow town (literally) called Coalinga. Coalinga was about half-way so, it was a good stopping point for the night. Before we came to our destination of the night we HAD to eat dinner in this Basque restaurant called The Woolgrowers. We make it a treat to dine at The Woolgrowers. It is almost a religious experience for me-well, as close to religion as it can be. We dined family style on a dinner of bread, green salad, potato salad, macaroni salad, soup, french fries, beans, lamb stew, and a main course consisting of either more lamb, prime rib or chicken. Those Basques really know how to eat. Oh, and for dessert, there was ice cream sundaes which I so femininely passed on; after all, I was watching my figure.

After the marathon dinner, we waddled out and eventually made it an hour down the road to Coalinga. We stayed in a Motel 6 and we slept like babies. I swear, Motel 6 is very cheap but I think it gets a bad rap. I mean, don't get me wrong, I am the luver of nice places to stay but I think that for the situation Motel 6 was more than adequate.

On the road again at 7 a.m. because it was supposed to something like 107 degrees and we wanted to get the majority of the trip completed before noon. I was the lucky one because my dad said that since I had long legs, I was to ride in the front seat all of the time. No complaints were heard out of me since I knew the back seat didn't have air conditioning. Poor saps in the back seat.

About 11:00, we stopped in Los Angeles for lunch. After feasting on a breakfast of rotting nectarines that my mom insisted we eat (we threw them out the window when my mom wasn't looking and blamed the window noise it makes on getting out those darn flies out), we were pretty hungry. We stopped at McDonald's and I proceeded to order a McGrill and a McFlurry (constantly watching television in the hospital, I became savvy with McDonald's lingo). When I got the McGrill, I found that it had sauce on it. Horrors. I cursed to myself and basically made a mountain out of a molehill. Thank

God my mom was there and fixed the problem by simply scraping off the sauce. Good ol' Mom. Despite my misgivings over lunch, I came to one conclusion. You can be taken to some of the best restaurants in the world, but as for a good meal, I don't think you can beat a $5 one at McDonald's.

After lunch, we had to meet one of Karin's friends to take her to San Diego with us. She was staying, of all places, at the Disneyland Hotel. I don't mean to sound snobby but I think that I will so, I will come to terms with it. When Karin and I heard that she was staying at the Disneyland Hotel, we erupted in paroxysms of disgust. We have only been to Disneyland once in our life and I think we were a little too old or we are just ultra-jaded. I was in the 9th grade and Karin was in the 3rd grade. I wasn't so repulsed by it but Karin was another story. She was really in disgust. We, both, were sickened by the obvious extravagant, over-commercialism (for instance, a pen cost $4), the flocking of people to rides that were obviously unsanitary, and the multitudes of overweight people. We, frankly, didn't think this was a good way to spend a vacation. I guess you could say Karin and I, at this or that point in our lives, are and were already snoots. So, when I say we recoiled in horror at the thought of one of Karin's friends staying there, you will understand why.

We got through with lunch and met Kristen (Karin's friend) at the Disneyland Hotel. I finally understood why they made this mecca to Disneyland. Kristen had an 11-year old sister who had never been to Disneyland. I thought this was noble of her parents and I prayed to God that their trips in the future wouldn't be as boring as this one.

The Michner's were very interesting and nice. The great uncle of Kristen was none other than the great, James A. Michner, one of my idols. Karin met Kristen at the fancy High School that she went to.

When we got to the Disneyland Hotel, I HAD to go to the bathroom. Since our car was packed to the brim with rim, we had to use one of the Disneyland Hotel's rickety wheelchairs. I won't even go into that. But when I talk about our car, it was really packed. I mean, it was really packed. I know I am straying off the subject but let me explain how packed the car was. First of all, you could not see out the back window because the view was obstructed by ice coolers, beach rafts, life preservers, a portable, outdoor barbeque, and sleeping pads-of all kinds. We didn't need 90% of this crap but... we felt compelled to bring all of the stuff. How good could a vacation be without 90% of your baggage being completely extraneous?

The vision situation was so bad that I had to yell "Proceed!" when my dad wanted to get over to the right and my mom, who was sitting on the left side in the back seat, yelled it when my dad wanted to get over to the left. I decided to make the distinction between "Go" and "Don't Go" by changing "Go" to "Proceed", just in case there was any confusion. I thought that "Go" and "Don't Go" were a little ambiguous so I clarified it. As you can probably tell, we had way, way too much time on our hands when we are in the car.

Back to the point now, I was saying that I HAD to go to the bathroom. We eventually extricated ourselves from the over packed car and making sure not to touch anything (heaven forbid we catch anything from those disdainful Disneylanders), Karin and I made our way to the bathroom. Thank God, there was only an hour and a half left of the drive.

Back from the restroom only left us confronted with another problem. When we were so intricately packing the car, we failed to take into consideration Kristen's things. Kristen had a rather large suitcase and we had no place to put it. Again, I wasn't too worried because I was riding shotgun and I didn't have worries like those peons in the back seat. We ended up tying Kristen's suitcase to the roof. I swear, it was such an oakie rig. We looked like something straight out of National Ampoons Vacation. Yep, going down the road was the Kryski Family masquerading as the Grizwald Family.

We left the parking lot in this manner; with a backfire to boot. It was San Diego or bust. I sunk down in my seat and pulled a hat down over my eyes, just in case there was somebody that I knew down in Southern California.

When we finally pulled into our hotel, we were sufficiently blown away. It was actually in La Jolla-a little suburb of San Diego. Boy, was the hotel nice. Apart from having its own golf course, croquet course, and tennis courts, it was right on the beach AND had it's own pool and Jacuzzi. We were like a type of country folk that had never seen anything nice. We were going around touching everything and lots of "Ohhs" and "Ahhs" were heard from us. I tell you, you can dress us up but you can't take us anywhere.

The only problem with the room was that it said it was handicapped accessible but in reality... it wasn't. The bathroom was fine. Better than fine, it was a dream except (always an except) there wasn't enough counter space to put all of the girls' crap on. There was no problem with handicapped accessibility for the disabled but this (the lack of sufficient counter space) handicapped us girls in our own little way. I say girls because really, there was only one guy-my dad. He always says, "These girls are going to gang up on me!". But he luvs it. But as I was saying, the room and surroundings weren't all handicapped accessible. The bed in the main room (which my parents occupied but I took plenty of naps in) didn't have enough space to fit a wheelchair in on the sides between the bed and the wall so, I had to transfer onto the foot of the bed and then shimmy myself into sleeping position by planting my feet and pushing upwards until I reached the head of the bed. I tell you, I was ready for a nap when all of the preparing for the nap was finished.

I said that my parents took the main bedroom. Karin and Kristen took the pull out couch so, where did that leave me? Well, I was relegated to a cot in the kitchen. I am so lucky! The cot was too short so, my feet hung off the end. All in all, the sight was pretty pitiful. That is where I lived for one week of my life. Correct me if I am wrong, but that doesn't sound like conditions fit for a princess?

We were going to meet our good friends, the Ritchie's, of ours when we were there . I think I've already told you this but you are going to hear it again. I like telling it, so bear with me. They have a house in La Jolla that has not 1, not 2, not 3, not 4, but 5 stories. You may ask, Janie, how do you get around in the house? Being that you are in a wheelchair and all. I would reply to this query by loftily saying, "Oh, I take the elevator". Like it's every day that I ride the elevator to gaze at the stars (one of the levels is on the roof and when there is a meteor shower, it is spectacular). Now THOSE are conditions fit for a princess. I could get very used to this life. Too bad it's not my own.

The day after our arrival the Ritchie's said they were going to take us to someplace called the Turf Club at the Marina del Mar race tracks. My mom and sister are really into horses and the Ritchie's heard this and suggested we go to the races one day. The next day, we got ready to go. We just wanted to go to the race tracks and gawk like normal tourists but the Ritchie's said we had to wear dresses that covered our shoulders and my dad had to wear a coat and tie. My dad didn't have a coat or a tie, I mean, we were on vacation at the beach! But luckily, Aaron came to my father's rescue and loaned my father a coat and tie. We all commented on how good my dad looked. I was wondering if Aaron would miss the coat and tie if it wasn't returned. All of us piled in our Chevy Tahoe and we followed the much sleeker Rolls Royce that held the Ritchie's. When we finally got to the tracks, we were ushered to a VIP parking lot. We knew we were, at that point, running with the big dogs because we parked among the BMW's and Mercedes's. The parking lot was enough to floor us; what about inside?

It was all fine and dandy up until that point. One of the elevators was broken so, since there was only one other, everybody and their brothers wanted to go upstairs with this one. I could not take the stairs like everybody in my party wanted to so, to be the courteous person that I am, I told everybody else to go ahead while my mom and I stayed back to wait for the unhurried elevator.

When we finally got up there (to the 8th floor), a half an hour later I might add, we discovered that it was very ritzy. There were ladies in hats and gloves; we were at the bottom of the barrel when it came to our pieced together garb. But betting on the races was fun! On this one race, the horse clearly had a French name. Edward asked me what it meant. I replied, "The Good Times Roll"; Edward went back to bet on him. The next thing I knew, Edward was thrusting $40 in my direction. I asked what that was for and Edward answered that it was for my knowledge of French. I guess, Edward bet $2 on The Good Times Roll and he had 1 to 10 odds and he won! It was because of Edward's generosity that I came to occupy $40. He bet on the horse and then decided to give the winnings to me because I helped him decipher the name. We joked that we would use the winnings to help fund a vacation. He suggested the Caribbean and I said it would be fun... but... there was no disabled access so, we would have to keep it quasi-national. I countered his suggestion with Hawaii. I told him that I fell in luv with Hawaii and that would be the only place that I would even consider going. It was all a big joke, though, wouldn't I enjoy that!

It was time to see the horses. You HAD to make the trip down to the starting gates to admire the horses. We could see, from our high perch, that there were brown ones, gray ones, black ones, and whatever else floated your boat. My mom and sister were having a serious discussion on the color or breed or gender of one. It went something like this:

"I think that one is a bay, gelding, thoroughbred, that is named Runs Like The Wind."

"No mom, I think that one is a sorrel, mare, thoroughbred, that is named As Fast As A Car."

The only way to solve the dispute was to make the voyage down and check it out. The only problem was that there was only 1 elevator working and it would have taken too long with me to get down there. I so graciously said that I really didn't care to see the horses. When in all reality, I would have luved to have seen the horses. They all made the trek down there while I stayed upstairs. I really am diplomatic, aren't I?

When they finally got back upstairs, and my mom and sister's dispute was settled, I was bursting at the seams. I am saying I had to urinate. You know go peepee, pee, to the bathroom, piss, and so on. I have a thing with my bladder that day it was Hell. It couldn't have picked a worse day to choose to act up. The bathroom was located in one corner and our table was in the complete other corner. That wasn't so bad except that we (my mom and I; we are a team; high 5) had to ask about 30 people to move. And this happened 3 times! When you have got to go, you have got to go. And this situation was no exception to the rule.

The rest of the day was basically uneventful except (I told you, always an except) for getting back down. That was 8 flights of stairs. Not 7, not 6, not 5, oh Hell, you can take my word for it. It was another half an hour getting down. I don't mind waiting, but I didn't want anybody else to have to wait with me. I am just extra sensitive that way, I guess. You see, I know it takes me a long time to do everything, so I don't mind waiting. But I hate everybody else to wait. Of course, they did wait and when we finally got down, we found ourselves in the middle of a mass exodus.

I've found one thing in my 3 years of being in a wheelchair. And that is, people don't pay attention to where they're going. For instance, leaving the tracks should have been fairly easy enough. But that is where you are mistaken; it is a nightmare in disguise. That is if you are in a wheelchair. People tend to look right in front of them-not to the side, or up, and certainly not down. After a few bloodied knees of the quasi-innocent tourists (serves them right; look where you are going), we made it to the car. Then, to start the trip back to our hotel where I was to curl up in my nice, soft cot. Obvious sarcasm.

I needed my beauty rest because the next day I had a rendezvous with Lee. Oh yes, Lee. Let me tell you about Lee.

Lee and I had a thing back in college. It wasn't "hot" or anything like that but it had something. Something...

I emailed Lee before we left because he lives in Poway, a suburb of San Diego. It would be the first time I'd seen him in 3 years. In other words, he hadn't seen me yet post-stroke. I was a bundle of nerves. I must say, I looked good. You hear that, Lee, I look damn good. I had on a green, sleeveless mock turtleneck with white Capri pants and white, leather Keds. Did I already mention I looked good? Fantastic? Hot?

We had the time all set for 7:30 at my hotel. And you know what? He didn't show. I was all pissed off but when we got home there was a message from him saying that he didn't know what was going on. Is that a polite way of saying, "I forgot"? Well, I'm glad, now in retrospect, because we ended up going to this place called George's. The wheelchair access was humiliating. Just humiliating. To get into the restaurant there was a flight of stairs and I didn't have my brace on so I couldn't walk them. Instead, I had to take the elevator. But finding the elevator was one thing and then another to take it. When we finally found it, it was outside and only two people could fit in it. When I say outside, I don't mean that there was an actual elevator located outside. I mean a 3-sided compartment that was outside the front of the building so, everybody who passed by could see the freak in the wheelchair getting hoisted up to eat dinner. It was so demeaning. I mean to say that it was one of the most humbling experiences of my entire life. When I say I'm glad Lee wasn't there, you will take my word for it.

Dinner was good, though. The place had a fantastic view but, unfortunately, it was dark. That's what happens when you go out for dinner. But that was ok by me because there was a window to look out but unfortunately again, it was just a smidgen too high for me to see out of in the chair. I tell you, the world has one big conspiracy against people in wheelchairs.

After dinner, we descended in the hideous elevator-type thing and then proceeded back to the hotel where I curled up on my little cot to be ready to face the day anew.

The next day I had my good friend, Jenn Palmer, who had a job in San Diego, was coming to have brunch with me. Instead of going to the hotel restaurant, my mother prepared us breakfast at a table placed in front of our room overlooking the ocean. It was really breathtaking. After breakfast, we decided to do a little boogie boarding. I thought that would be ok since, the surf was so calm in Hawaii. Boy, was I wrong. It was very different in San Diego. My dad accompanied us (the old faithful that he is; he doesn't want his baby hurt) and we made our way out to the waves. Jenn and I were giddy as though we had never done this before.

When a good sized wave was coming, Jenn yelled, "Go!". That did it. I started frantically kicking and my right hand came off of the board. I had on a life jacket and the board was connected to a cable that was then tied around my wrist, so I didn't lose the board. I became totally discumbooberated and began swimming for my dear life. Of course, I was swimming the wrong way. I was swimming towards the bottom of the ocean. I didn't know which way was up, and I was running out of air.

It was about this time that I heard my dad yelled, "Hold On!". He proceeded to pull me all of the way back to shore. I swear, I must have looked like a corpse floating there with my face down, my hair floating around my head, my dad frantically trying to make it to shore, and my boogie board still attached to my wrist all the while getting battered by the surf. On shore, as I furiously tried to get my breath, Karin and Kristen, who had been watching my endeavor from the shore, ran up to me and said, "Jane, Are you ok? We saw you, and we thought that must have hurt". A brilliant deduction, girls. You are so smart.

About this time, Jenn sauntered up and said, "Knarley waves, dude". I suddenly became very concerned about her becoming a "So Cal" girl and forgetting about her "Nor Cal" roots. What was the deal with the lingo?

As for me, I was done for the day. I declared that I didn't like San Diego, and I much preferred Hawaii. My boogie boarding experience was a flop and I decided to stay out of the ocean.

Instead, we decided to sun ourselves. Bright idea. Jenn has some Italian in her and me... well, I have all Northern European roots in me. I can stay out 10 minutes and after that I am looking like a lobster. Jenn, on the other hand, can stay out in the sun all day and not be affected in any way, except for a great tan. That day it was kind of over cast so, it was cooler than normal. Like the dummy that I am, I stayed out one whole hour. Death for me. Since I can't easily roll over on my stomach, I tanned/burned on my back. Consequently, I was "two-toned". I looked like a lobster on front and an albino in back. It was quite fetching.

Jenn and I said our good-byes, not by kissing and hugging, rather by blowing air kisses. Hugging would have hurt just too darned much.

That night we were going to the Ritchie's house for a dinner party. I decided to invite my big sister in my sorority, Sasha, who lives in San Diego with her husband. Let me tell you about Sasha. She is the most wild and crazy girl you can imagine. There are no words to express how crazy she is. I don't even remember how we got hooked up but she has been a lot of fun. For some reason, she thinks I am as crazy as her; I am as straight as a board, but I let her think whatever she wants. Take for instance, I flew down to San Diego for her wedding. Not an out-there thing to do, a good friend was getting married and I wanted to be there. She was just speechless that I came. I guess, she thought that since I was in a wheelchair (I had the glorious gift of having my hemorrhage by then), I wouldn't come. But I did. That was just another example of how utterly crazy Jane is.

Well, I emailed Sasha before going down to San Diego and we decided on that specific night to go out. When she came to pick me up and go to the Ritchie's, she was driving a rather expensive car. Her father had just died and I gather that he had quite a bit of money. Since her mother wasn't in the picture and

132

it was only her brother and her, she fell heir to it. When I commented on how nice her car was, she blithely said that Justin (her husband) had never had a new car and she just surprised him with it one day.

I thought, nice surprise.

When we got to the Ritchie's, they had a full-on spread laid out on the 5th floor. That would be the roof, but oh, don't you worry. Remember, they have an elevator.

San Diego is really close to the Mexican border, hence you get a good deal of Mexicans working there. Sasha and I were up on the roof and there is this Mexican worker up there and Sasha starts this in depth conversation with him- in Spanish. It turns out that Sasha is fully fluent in Spanish. Boy, did I feel stupid.

All I could say was, "Como Estas!". I just used Sasha as an interpreter. They could have been talking smack about me and I wouldn't have known it. That is one downside of French. Nobody speaks it in California. Maybe, just maybe, I chose the wrong language. Maybe I could start over. Maybe not. Have too much time in on French.

Dinner was fantastic, fabulous, superb... need I go on. Shall we say it was good? It consisted of chicken, salmon, filet mingon, pasta, bread, salad, and more. It was so delicious that it masked my memory bank. I can't even remember!

When we went to leave, Sasha and I took off early. Of course, we got lost. Between a San Diego native and someone who was staying at the destination we were trying to reach, we showed a poor display of knowledge of the area. It was pretty bad. We were in downtown La Jolla, and we didn't know where we were going. So, Sasha asked these 3 guys how to get there. They knew the surrounding area as well us. Or so we thought. They sent us on this wild goose chase, all over Hell and gone. I was wondering what we were going to do.

Oh look, here are the guys again. We had made a circle. What does Sasha do? She rolled down the window and yelled, "What's up you guys? We are still lost!".

As I sunk down lower in my seat, the guys tried to figure out what went wrong. When they were sure they had given us the right directions, we were off once more. These directions fared as well as the last ones. We ended up asking this really handsome German-American guy for directions. He had a map and everything. I was wondering if he needed any tutoring sessions for his English. Because I knew just the person.

We ended up refinding the place but arrived after my parents. Sasha left, but she was returning the next night for dinner on the beach. After she left, I curled up on my cot-in the corner of the kitchen. By this time, the whole cot thing was getting old. I have rights, you know.

\\\

I wasn't too jazzed about anything, let alone dinner, on the beach. To get to the beach, you have to climb up and over this wave break. You see, it was all concrete and then this wave break and then ocean. To get up and over the wave break, I had to have the assistance of my father. I could probably do it all on my own considering there was a hand rail (and there was) but my mother and sister wouldn't hear of it. My mom's favorite line is, "I've spent all of this time and effort...".

I just liked to hear them fuss a little, so every now and then I'd start up the wave break. Is that cruel?

Sasha arrived and we made our way to the beach. Chuck, who is 26 and my older brother, came down for the weekend. He had just broken up with his girlfriend of 14 months so, he was on the prowl. Well, he didn't come alone. Oh no, he had a girl with him. She was 18 (are alarm bells going off in your head). You're right! I am younger than Chuck and this chick was younger than me. Hmmm, can we say rebound? Sasha just looked at me when she met her and rolled her eyes. On top of being 18 (which I didn't like if you haven't noticed), she was working a piece of gum like you wouldn't believe. I thought she was joking at first because my mother and I always joke about people chewing gum. I almost asked, "Did my mother put you up to this?". But after I met her, I'm glad I didn't.

At dinner, there were two tables because of our large group. On sand you, obviously, can't roll as well as you can on the ideal-concrete. Sasha and I ended up sitting at the grown-up table. The grown-up table wasn't too bad, but every now and then we'd hear a whoop and look over to see some antics going on where all of the younger people were sitting. At least, I wasn't sitting there because I knew the scenario. You would be talking to somebody who has had one or two drinks and when that somebody thought they were done talking would get up and leave-whether or not they were really done talking. Did I happen to that there was a good deal of rum being consumed? I am talking at the, yes, the kid's table. That is my pet peave; when somebody has a little to drink and they are talking to you one minute and then the next, they are off doing something new. There are 3 reasons why I don't excessively drink: 1) I don't want to be known as the drunk girl in the wheelchair 2) my voice is slow enough without alcohol 3) for the latter stated.

I ended up sitting at the adult table and I enjoyed myself even though the whoops at the younger people's table were getting louder as the night progressed. And as I stated before, the sand wasn't too easy to move the wheelchair in so, Sasha and I stayed in place. Instead, we enjoyed a scintillating conversation about the homosexuality of the ancient Romans. Just ask me anything about the homosexuality of the ancient Romans and I will tell you. I could see that Sasha really wanted to go over to the kid's table, but as a good friend, she stayed with me. We had to speak up as the night progressed due to the increasing volume of the table next to ours.

When Sasha left, we blew air kisses too because my burn was not quite at the touching stage. This was going to be our last meeting for quite a while but I wasn't worried. Sasha would do something crazy like skateboard up to Nor-Cal.

The next day was our departure date. I, personally, liked Hawaii better than San Diego. In San Diego, at the resort we stayed at, there was an ever so slight incline to the walkways. It wouldn't have mattered to the average walking person, but as far as a walker and a wheelchair (remember, I was still in the manual chair); I need it completely flat. An incline one way or another wrecks havoc on me. I prefered Hawaii where it was all level, the water was warmer, there were no waves, and come on people; it was Hawaii.

We set out, once more, me in the front, and the peons in the back. I was silently laughing as the cool air conditioner blew on me. But we still had lunch with Great Aunt Betty.

Let me tell you about Great Aunt Betty. My grandmother and her had a falling out some years back, the details are a little bit sketchy; I think on purpose. We, consequently, we did not see her much. In fact, I had never seen her once. But her husband just died and we felt bad for her-being in Santa Barbara all by herself and no kids. When we arrived at her place, the car was packed, again, with no room to spare, with the exception of the front seat, which had plenty of room. We wouldn't want to disturb the pretty, pretty princess, now would we?

Anyway, as I was saying, my dad had the car packed like we would never see tomorrow so, my sister and Kristen volunteered to walk me in. The Weanie Walker was underneath all kinds of crap. When I say crap, let me give you an example so you know what I'm talking about. It was under a coffee maker, a boogie board, a quasi-wet towel, and the top to a swimsuit (the bottoms being packed away in the wrong suitcase). Instead of unpacking all of this stuff, Karin and Kristen opted for walking me in solo.

Ok, I lean a lot into the left when I walk. That is why I prefer my dad to walk with me, because I can lean on him all I want. He is just an ox. We don't have him around for anything other than walking me! Karin and Kristen assumed position and started to walk me in. You would have thought I was trying to kill them or something. They moaned and groaned so, so much. I wanted to just say, "Hell with you!". But then again, I can't walk independently so the only place I could go was the ground and I wasn't too keen on that.

We finally got into Great Aunt Betty's house and we discovered that it was as clean as a whistle. I, for one, didn't want to disturb anything. I wanted to stand up because my bumm was starting to hurt-a little too much sitting can wreck havoc on the ass. My dad took over the walking when we entered the house and he steered me over to a bare wall. We them engaged in polite conversation with Great Aunt Betty while I stood propped against a wall. It was quaint.

For lunch, we decided to go into town. I relieved Karin and Kristen of the duty of walking me and instead I went with good old reliable dad. My dad took the wheel as always and my mom rode with Great Aunt Betty in her ancient, convertible Rabbit (a totally uncharacteristic car for prim and proper Great Aunt Betty). My dad was kind of fogging around and as we were pulling out of Great Aunt Betty's driveway we ran over a garbage can in the ground. Great Aunt Betty didn't see so, we just acted like it didn't happen. Later, my mother was inquiring about the smell around the front of the car and my dad broke down and told her. Leave it to my mom to figure something like that out. You can't get much by my mother. My father, yes but my mom, nope.

When we reached this place that we were going to eat at, I insisted that my parents pull out the wheelchair because I just wasn't going to do a repeat of Great Aunt Betty's house. We were all seated at a circular table and it went Karin, Great Aunt Betty, my mom, me, my dad, and Kristen. I was sitting as far away from Great Aunt Betty as possible. You have to understand that you can understand me just perfectly one on one when there is no background noise. But if there is background noise like in, say for instance, a crowded restaurant, you really can't hear me unless you have excellent hearing. Great Aunt Betty, being circa 75, did not have excellent hearing. Therefore, I do not know my Great Aunt Betty as well as I'd like to. It's not as though I didn't try-on the contrary. But I thought my witticisms were falling on a deaf ear (literally) so, I thought it best to just shut up. Which I did-taking the hint from my mom's kick from under the table. Oh well!

I was a little bit miffed because, let's be truthful, I am always EVERYBODY'S favorite. A while later, Karin received a package in the mail from Great Aunt Betty. It was a package of cucumber seeds. It turns out that Karin asked Great Aunt Betty for her cucumbers because Karin luvs her cucumbers. At home, when she received her package in the mail, Karin was jubilant at her newfound admirer and she couldn't help but rub in that she was someone's favorite this time. Well, screw Karin.

After lunch, we decided to make a straight shot home. That was only 6 hours in the car not to mention all of the time already spent in the car that day without being able to lay back and relieve some of the pressure on my bumm. When I got home, my family and Kristen had to unfold me and very carefully lay me on my bed.

It took me about 5 days to recover from that car ride and trip. Oh well, I guess one brilliant guy once said, "You roll with the punches". Who ever said he was brilliant?

I pondered my summer of vacations. It wasn't TOO bad except for the breaking of the wheelchair. That was pretty bad.

I guess it's an ideal thought to have the world be handi-capped accessible. Wouldn't it be nice. But then again, who wants to live in a completely accessible world?

To tell you the truth, I would never have given a second thought to wheelchair accessibility if this whole brain hemor-rhage hadn't happened to me. In a way, you can think of it as a good thing... in a very morbid, perverse way of thinking. It has led me to become very introspective about the two worlds I have lived in-the walking world and the wheelchair world.

Malchance:
From Walking to a Wheelchair

By
Jane Kryski

Available at your local bookstore or use this page to order.
--1-932581-30-8- Malchance: From Walking to a Wheelchair
- $14.50 U.S

Send to: Trident Media Inc.
801 N. Pitt Street #123
Alexandria, VA 22314
Toll Free # 1-877-874-6334
Please send me the item above. I am enclosing
$_____(please add $4.50 per book to cover postage
and handling).
Send check, money order, or credit card:

Card #_____ Exp. date _____

Mr./Mrs./Ms._____
Address_____
City/State_____Zip_____

Please allow four to six weeks for delivery.
Prices and availability subject to change without notice.

Printed in the United States
95615LV00004B/88-96/A